ALL THE REASONS WHY HILLARY JUST ISN'T RIGHT

THOMAS WILLIAMS

SOURCEBOOKS HYSTERIA™
AN IMPRINT OF SOURCEBOOKS, INC.®
NAPERVILLE, ILLINOIS

Sourcebooks and the colophon are registered trademarks of Sourcebooks, Inc.

Published by Sourcebooks Hysteria, an imprint of Sourcebooks, Inc.
P.O. Box 4410, Naperville, Illinois 60567-4410
(630) 961-3900
Fax: (630) 961-2168
www.sourcebooks.com

Library of Congress Cataloging-in-Publication Data

Williams, Thomas.
  I hate Hillary : all the reasons why Hillary just isn't right / Thomas Williams.
     p. cm.
  Includes bibliographical references.
  ISBN 978-1-4022-1306-9 (trade pbk.)
  1. Clinton, Hillary Rodham—Political and social views. 2. Clinton, Hillary Rodham—Ethics. 3. Clinton, Hillary Rodham—Humor. 4. Clinton, Hillary Rodham—Miscellanea. 5. Presidents—United States—Election—2008. 6. Women presidential candidates—United States—Biography—Miscellanea. 7. Presidential candidates—United States—Biography—Miscellanea. 8. Presidents' spouses—United States—Biography—Miscellanea. 9. Women legislators—United States—Biography—Miscellanea. I. Title.

E887.C55W55 2008
973.929092--dc22

                              2007051840

           Printed and bound in the United States of America.
                    VP 10 9 8 7 6 5 4 3 2 1

CONTENTS

★ ★ ★ ★ ★ ★ ★ ★ ★ ★ ★ ★ ★ ★ ★ ★

Part 2: This 'n That

INTRODUCTION

★ ★ ★ ★ ★ ★ ★ ★ ★ ★ ★ ★ ★ ★ ★ ★ ★

As the story goes, there's this photographer who's at the end of his career, and he hasn't taken that Pulitzer Prize-winning photograph he's yearned to take all his life, so he decides to leave his job and use the money he has saved to travel the world in hopes of taking that one great shot.

One day, he's in one of the many worldwide locations he's visiting, in his hotel room, when not far from his window, he sees an immense dam rupture and the area around the hotel start to flood. He runs and gets his camera, but before he can load it he sees a hand, then an arm, then a head rise out of the water. It's Hillary Clinton! She keeps stretching towards him . . . and he has five to ten seconds to grab her hand and save her. He now faces one of the worst dilemmas of his life . . . namely, should he use color or black and white film?

Implicit in the joke above is a big truth about the woman named Hillary Diane Rodham Clinton, who at this writing is making a run to become President of the United States. The truth is this: Many people hate her. But within those sentiments lies this question: Why? She seems pleasant enough, well dressed, nice looking, always smiling, outgoing, throwing off a witty line here and there, standing by Bill when he needed her, loving her daughter Chelsea, and trying to help Americans, particularly the poor, disadvantaged and minorities.

This book will show why people hate her—and how much (a lot!). Indeed, a couple of people writing on the Internet hate Hillary so much, some of their readers called the Secret Service to investigate threats they made toward Hillary. As you will see, some of the hatred is profound.

This book is divided into two parts. Part I, The Heart of Darkness, explores why Hillary does what she does, what she is, and how she developed into the person she is—a person who is devious, power mad, crude, and vicious. While Part I does not pretend to be a psychological tome, it does bring up some explanations to why Hillary is the way she is. It explains how she changed from a teenager living in a quiet, tree-lined conservative town in Illinois into someone whose fundamental philosophy is socialistic—someone who will do virtually anything to win, and someone who could actively help an outfit like the Black Panthers, a violent and murderous group in their heyday. And it also looks at some of the implications of her elected position, and what she did to get there.

While the style of this book may sound more academic than popular in style, it is not. I have tried to make it as entertaining as possible. To do this, the book contains a host of sidebars, which contain snapshots of her behavior. Hopefully these will add up to a mosaic that will reveal her in all her smarmy glory.

Part II of this book is more overtly entertaining. It contains some hilarious Bill and Hillary jokes and stories, a roundup of anti-Hillary merchandise (our favorite is a nutcracker) and the last chapter—Chapter 10—might also be called "Bloggers Gone Wild," where people show their pure hatred for her. There is also a detailed "Gruesome Glossary" which can give someone a quick grasp of Hillary's life and how she's conducted it.

Overall, I have tried to keep the content light and entertaining, though the truth is that sometimes my research revealed facts about HRC that are not entertaining at all, and pissed me off greatly.

I hope you enjoy this book, and that it adds to your savvy about the creature known as Hillary.

—Thomas Williams

PART 1
The Heart of Darkness

CHAPTER 1

Hillary the Bizarre

★ ★ ★ ★ ★ ★ ★ ★ ★ ★ ★ ★ ★ ★ ★ ★ ★

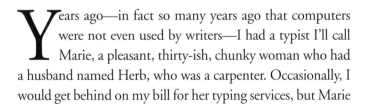

"She had defended a man—
for the wrong reason—who perhaps
99 out of **100** women would have left."

—Thomas Williams

Years ago—in fact so many years ago that computers were not even used by writers—I had a typist I'll call Marie, a pleasant, thirty-ish, chunky woman who had a husband named Herb, who was a carpenter. Occasionally, I would get behind on my bill for her typing services, but Marie did not seem to mind. She was very easygoing. She'd usually say something like: "Whenever you can pay, Tom, that's fine."

I got to be friendly with her, and one day we sat down at the kitchen table to have a cup of coffee. The conversation somehow drifted to adultery, and I expressed my feelings about it, telling her it would devastate me if my wife cheated on me. Then she told me her feelings about Herb, "If I caught Herb cheating on me, I'd pin him to the mattress."

I was puzzled. "What do you mean? Is that a wrestling hold or something?"

"No," she said, and demonstrated. She held the fist of one hand high simulating holding something and then drove it swiftly down towards the table. I realized it was a knife. All I could think to say was, "Listen, Marie, I'm going to catch up on my bill ASAP, okay?"

Marie's reaction to her husband possibly cheating on her is not that unusual for a woman or man. Homicides occur all the time because adultery is a stake in the heart of a marriage. It basically tells your mate that you don't care about him or her, that you are untrustworthy, and that a marriage vow doesn't matter. Statistically, about 18 percent of the population commits adultery; and without scientifically measuring it, it seems that many of these couples stay together, but the marriage is really over. Love is all about caring, and adultery destroys that. Never again will one party trust the other; never again will they believe, down deep, that they really care about the other person. There will always be the nagging question: Will they do it again?

We're talking here, of course, of cheating that happens just once. But what if it happens more than once—or many times? Or hundreds of times? What would that do to the heart and soul of a normal woman? It would kill her, in a sense, and the only way she could possibly stay with that person would be if she felt threatened, if she was married to a psychopath who would hurt her if she left him, if she had some deep-seated need to be abused, or, if she had an agenda that was bigger, more important than her husband cheating on her..

Which brings us to the Clintons.

William Jefferson Clinton, 42nd president of the United States, grew up dirt poor in Arkansas, and his father abandoned the family when he was a little boy. Clinton often saw his heavily made up and floridly dressed mother go out with many different men. That basic background produced a man who, one might say, has a perpetual erection.

One of the characteristics of someone like this, psychologists say, is that they will take great risks for sex. When one looks at Clinton's behavior as a public official, it's easy to see he took many risks for sex that could have generated a scandal that would bring him crashing down from the high perches that he had achieved in his home state of Arkansas, first as attorney general, then governor. And it says something about how obsessed he was.

There are many examples of Clinton acting out this obsession. In his book, *The Seduction of Hillary Rodham Clinton*, author David Brock says that while Clinton was

Arkansas governor, state troopers Roger Perry and Larry Patterson wrote in their book about their years guarding Clinton that he "had been prone to extramarital affairs, conducting several at a time, as well as indulging in numerous one-night stands." The troopers alleged that, while they were being paid by the state and driving state cars, they were regularly instructed by Clinton to approach women and to solicit their telephone numbers," then to drive them to rendezvous points and stand guard during sexual encounters. No doubt the most infamous of these was with Paula Jones, though it didn't culminate in a sex act. The troopers brought her to a Little Rock hotel where the governor was waiting. Indeed he was. When Ms. Jones entered the room, Clinton was standing there with his pants and underwear pooled down around his ankles and with an erect penis. (It turned out to be an expensive erection. Ultimately Clinton settled out of court with Jones for $850,000 for sexual assault.)

"The troopers further alleged," Brock said, "that they were eyewitness to some of the encounters, including incidents where oral sex was performed on Clinton on the grounds of the governor's mansion and in the parking lot of a local elementary school."

Another trooper, L.D. Brown, said that while he worked at the Governor's mansion in the mid-'80s, he also solicited sexual partners during Clinton's travels throughout the state. "Over a hundred at least," Brown said. "I'd hate to even try to guess."

Of course, Bill Clinton didn't become a sex fiend as an adult. It started when he was a little boy, and continued through high school and into college. He was in full Satyr-like tilt when he met Hillary at Yale Law School in the '70s.

Larry Flynt's Offer

Gennifer Flowers posed nude in Playboy. Hustler publisher Larry Flynt is said to have offered Hillary one million dollars to take off her clothes in his magazine. And five million dollars to keep them on.

–Anon

"'You know, if I were a single man, I might ask that mummy out,' said President Bill Clinton while looking at 'Juanita,' a newly discovered Incan mummy on display at the National Geographic Museum. 'Probably she does look good compared to the mummy he's been fucking.'"

—Mike McCurry, ex-White House Press Secretary, making an off-the-cuff joke to reporters.

★ ★ ★ ★ ★ ★ ★ ★ ★ ★ ★ ★ ★ ★ ★ ★

The Secret Service Knew Too, of Course

The Secret Service of course knew that Clinton was a sex fiend. A number of years ago I had the chance to talk with a Secret Service agent who had guarded Clinton and had recently retired. He showed me a picture of himself shaking hands with Bill Clinton on that day, and standing next to the agent was his attractive blonde wife. "You know," the agent said, "while Bill was shaking my hand he was glomming my wife."

★ ★ ★ ★ ★ ★ ★ ★ ★ ★ ★ ★ ★ ★ ★ ★

A number of writers have said that Hillary didn't seem to care about sex one way or the other. Bill not only cared but had rented a house that was convenient for his sexual soireés and the tall, good-looking, witty, brilliant guy had an endless array of women coming to the house, drawn there like iron filings to a magnet.

Hillary had to know about his sexual hijinks. As one of her close friends said, "She always knew what was going on around her."

And therein lies the rub. Why did she tolerate these sexcapades? Why didn't she leave him? He was constantly eroding the bedrock of their relationship. And what did she do? She endured it.

Why?

The simple answer, research indicates, is aching, unfulfilled ambition. All her life, Hillary, like Bill, had been longing to get to the top of what might be called Mount Achievement. She had to see Bill—though this sounds incredibly shortsighted in terms of ultimate happiness—as someone who would somehow help her get to that high place. She hitched her wagon to a superstar. Indeed, since Bill was seven years old—and Hillary knew this—he had told the world that he wanted to be President of the United States. Ironically, his hero was John F. Kennedy, also a world-class adulterer. And together, as Edward Klein says in his book *The Truth About Hillary*, they had first started to plan for his presidential run in 1982, ten years before he actually threw his hat in the ring.

Just how far would Hillary go to keep her dreams of glory and power intact?

She had looked the other way when Bill cohabited with everything in Arkansas except the razorback pigs (maybe). The answer became clear in February 1992, while Hillary and Bill campaigned their way across the picturesque, snow-covered landscape of New Hampshire. While they were trying to win that state's presidential primary, the equivalent of a grenade rolled into their campaign. A glossy cabaret singer named Gennifer Flowers alleged that she had a twelve-year affair with Bill Clinton, not only while he was a bigwig in Arkansas politics but also while he was married to Hillary.

Clinton vociferously denied it, but Flowers had some nasty proof: tapes of her and Clinton in their lovebird days. Hillary immediately went into a defensive mode. Indeed, almost ridiculously, when the media questioned Hillary about why she thought Bill and Gennifer referred to each other as "honey," she explained that was a common way the people of Arkansas referred to one another, and it had nothing to do with romantic intimacy.

But Flowers wouldn't go away, and then Hillary revealed the depths of her own achievement agenda. With their presidential run about to disappear under an avalanche of bad publicity, she—they—agreed to talk about the Flowers accusation on *60 Minutes*, questioned by the pit bull clone of Mike Wallace, Steve Kroft.

The interview was conducted with Bill and Hillary subtly showing a united front, sitting next to one another on a couch.

Kroft, who would seemingly ask anyone anything, tried mightily to get Clinton to admit to indiscretions (See "The Clintons versus *60 Minutes*") but direct questions were met with sidesteps by both Clintons that would have made a world-class bullfighter nod in admiration. When it was all over, Kroft had not touched either of the Clintons.

★ ★ ★ ★ ★ ★ ★ ★ ★ ★ ★ ★ ★ ★ ★ ★ ★

The Clintons versus *60 Minutes*

Transcript of the Interview by Steve Kroft of the Clintons concerning Gennifer Flowers

Kroft: Who is Gennifer Flowers? Do you know her?

Bill Clinton: Oh, yes.

Kroft: How do you know her? How would you describe your relationship?

Bill Clinton: Very limited, but until this, you know, friendly but limited . . .

Kroft: Was she a friend, an acquaintance? Does your wife know her?

Hillary Clinton: Oh, sure.

Bill Clinton: Yes. She was an acquaintance; I would say a friendly acquaintance . . .

Kroft: She is alleging and has described in some detail in the supermarket tabloid what she calls a twelve-year affair with you.

Bill Clinton: That allegation is false.

Hillary Clinton: When this woman first got caught up in these charges, I felt as I've felt about all of these women: that they . . . had just been minding their own business and they got hit by a meteor . . . I felt terrible about what was

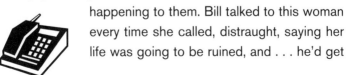

happening to them. Bill talked to this woman every time she called, distraught, saying her life was going to be ruined, and . . . he'd get off the phone and tell me that she said sort of wacky things, which we thought were attributable to the fact that she was terrified.

Bill Clinton: It was only when money came out, when the tabloid went down there offering people money to say that they had been involved with me, that she changed her story. There's a recession on.

Kroft: I'm assuming from your answer that you're categorically denying that you ever had an affair with Gennifer Flowers.

Bill Clinton: I said that before. And so has she.

Kroft: You've said that your marriage has had problems, that you've had difficulties. What do you mean by that? What does that mean? Is that some kind of—help us break the code. I mean, does that mean that you were separated? Does that mean that you had communication problems? Does that mean you contemplated divorce? Does it mean adultery?

Bill Clinton: I think the American people, at least people that have been married for a long time, know what it means and know the whole range of things it can mean.

TOP SECRET

Kroft: You've been saying all week that you've got to put this issue behind you. Are you prepared tonight to say that you've never had an extramarital affair?

Bill Clinton: I'm not prepared tonight to say that any married couple should ever discuss that with anyone but themselves. I'm not prepared to say that about anybody. I think that the . . .

Kroft: . . . That's what you've been saying essentially for the last couple of months.

Bill Clinton: . . . You go back and listen to what I've said. You know, I have acknowledged wrongdoing. I have acknowledged causing pain in my marriage. I have said things to you tonight and to the American people from the beginning that no American politician ever has.

I think most Americans who are watching this tonight, they'll know what we're saying; they'll get it, and they'll feel that we have been more candid. And I think what the press has to decide is: Are we going to engage in a game of "gotcha"? . . . I can remember a time when a divorced person couldn't run for president, and that time, thank goodness, has passed. Nobody's prejudiced against anybody because they're divorced. Are we going to take the reverse position now that if people have problems in their marriage and there are things in their past which they don't want to discuss which are painful to them, that they can't run?

Kroft: You're trying to put this issue behind you, and the problem with the answer is it's not a denial. And people are sitting out there—voters—and they're saying, "Look, it's really pretty simple. If he's never had an extramarital affair, why doesn't {he} say so?"

Bill Clinton: That may be what they're saying. You know what I think they're saying? I think they're saying, "Here's a guy who's leveling with us." . . . I've told the American {people} more than any other candidate for president. The result of that has been everybody going to my state and spending more time trying to play "gotcha."

Hillary Clinton: There isn't a person watching this who would feel comfortable sitting on this couch detailing everything that ever went on in their life or their marriage. And I think it's real dangerous in this country if we don't have some zone of privacy for everybody . . .

Kroft: . . . I agree with you that everyone wants to put this behind you. And the reason the problem has not gone away is because your answer is not a denial . . . .

Bill Clinton: Of course it's not. And let's take it from your point of view, that won't make it go away. I mean if you deny, then you have a whole other horde of people going down there offering more money and trying to prove that you lied. And if you say yes, then you have just what I have already said by being open and telling you that we have had problems. You have, "Oh good, now we can go play 'gotcha' and find out who it is."

Now, no matter what I say, to pretend that the press will then let this die, then we are kidding ourselves. I mean, you know, this has become a virtual cottage industry. The only way to put it behind us, I think, is for all of us to agree that this guy has told us about all we need to know. Anybody who is listening gets the drift of it and let's go on and get back to the real problems of this country . . . .

Kroft: . . . {The} question of marital infidelity is an issue with a sizable portion of the electorate. According to the latest CBS News poll . . . 14 percent of the registered voters in America wouldn't vote for a candidate who's had an extra-marital affair.

Bill Clinton: I know it's an issue, but what does that mean? That means that 86 percent of the American people either don't think it's relevant to presidential performance or look at whether a person, looking at all the facts, is the best to serve.

Kroft: I think most Americans would agree that it's very admirable that you've stayed together—that you've worked your problems out and that you've seemed to reach some sort of understanding and arrangement.

Bill Clinton: Wait a minute, wait a minute, wait a minute. You're looking at two people who love each other. This is not an arrangement or an understanding. This is a marriage. That's a very different thing.

Hillary Clinton: You know, I'm not sitting here—some little woman standing by my man like Tammy Wynette. I'm sitting here because I love him, and I respect him, and I honor what he's been through and what we've been through together. And you know, if that's not enough for people, then heck, don't vote for him.

Kroft: . . . One of your campaign advisers told us the other day, "Bill Clinton has got to level with the American people tonight, and otherwise his candidacy is dead." You feel like you've leveled with the American people?

Bill Clinton: I have absolutely leveled with the American people.

Kroft: . . . You came here tonight to try to put it behind you . . . Do you think you've succeeded?

Bill Clinton: That's up to the American people and to some extent up to the press. This will test the character of the press. It is not only my character that has been tested.

—Source: Washington Post

★ ★ ★ ★ ★ ★ ★ ★ ★ ★ ★ ★ ★ ★ ★ ★

Over the next few days it soon became obvious that the Clinton campaign could be taken off life support. Indeed, they could leave the hospital. In a very real way, Hillary had saved the campaign and her efforts would ultimately lead to a cold day in February 1993 in Washington D.C., where Bill Clinton placed his hand on, of all things, a Bible, and took the oath of office as he was sworn in as President of the Free World.

Never mind what *he* had done, ***think again of what she had done!*** She had defended a man that perhaps ninety-nine out of a hundred women would have left, and for the wrong reason—not as a latter-day Tammy Wynette standing by her man but, as it will play out in this book, to fill the void, the ache, the ferocious drive inside her that will never go away until she stands on top of Mount Achievement.

But the *60 Minutes* confrontation was by no means Hillary's grandest Tammy Wynette bit.

"President Clinton had quadruple bypass surgery over the weekend and is recovering nicely. The doctors told him he can resume having sex in about two weeks. And Hillary said, 'If he does, I'll kill him.'"

—David Letterman

"The Clinton Library is state of the art. They have a nice gift shop. You can buy a T-shirt. You can buy a coffee mug. You can also buy condoms with the presidential seal on them."

—David Letterman

★ ★ ★ ★ ★ ★ ★ ★ ★ ★ ★ ★ ★ ★ ★

Killed Her Cats?

Kathleen Willey is an attractive, one-time White House aide who in 1993 claimed to have been groped by then-president Bill Clinton in the Oval Office.

The *Fox and Friends* morning program detailed charges in the book *Target: Caught in the Crosshairs of Bill and Hillary Clinton* that Willey's cat, Bullseye, was the victim of a targeted hit by a Clinton-hired henchman.

Kathleen said, "A man, he was pretending to be a jogger, he came up to me and just asked did I ever find my cat? He mentioned my cat by name and [said], 'Yeah, that Bullseye was a really nice cat.'" Willey said that the abducted cat was part of an intimidation plan organized by the Clintons after she was called to testify in Paula Jones' sexual harassment suit against the president.

"But it didn't stop there," said Fox News host Brian Kilmeade. "Does the name Fluffy mean anything to you? A year later she bought a cat, named it Fluffy. That cat ended up dead as well underneath the porch. She thinks…the person who did this is linked back to Hillary."

★ ★ ★ ★ ★ ★ ★ ★ ★ ★ ★ ★ ★ ★ ★

Something else arose which required a reprise—something now known as "Monicagate." In this, a pretty, buxom intern in the White House named Monica Lewinsky had become smitten with Bill. She managed to get past a woman named Evelyn Lieberman who had actually been appointed by Hillary as a gatekeeper so young females couldn't get to what someone characterized as a "smiling satyr." But Monica loved Bill and succeeded in getting by Lieberman for thirty-something soireés within the Oval Office, which came to be known as the "Oral Office," both for the fellatio that Monica performed on the President and for his practice of lubricating his cigars by sticking them in her vagina and then sucking on them.

But then something happened that unraveled the affair and almost gave Clinton a one-way ticket back to Arkansas. Namely, his Hillary-appointed gatekeeper, Lieberman, found out that Lewinsky was involved in an affair with Bill, and the young girl was rapidly transferred out of the White House to a job at the Pentagon.

From that time on, Monica could not get access to the President who, when he started to cross paths with her in public functions, started to treat her as if she suffered from leprosy. Monica, all of twenty-one or twenty-two while she was involved with Bill, was crushed by the lack of attention he paid her and started referring to him as "The Big Creep."

She also started to talk to Pentagon coworker Linda Tripp, who encouraged the young girl to, as it were, "cry on her shoulder." Monica did, telling Linda about her relationship and including all kinds of prurient details, while Linda listened avidly and responded sympathetically.

But there was, as one observer said, "a turd in the punch bowl." Linda, spurred on by an atavistic literary agent, taped the conversations, ending up with twenty hours worth of tape, enough to write a book. She also gave copies of the tapes to Kenneth Starr, who had been appointed to investigate the Clintons' role in the Whitewater debacle (see Chapter 3: Lies and BS). Starr had expanded his investigation to the Lewinsky and Paula Jones affairs which involved Clinton lying under oath and making him vulnerable to impeachment.

In the midst of all this, Hillary Clinton had been scheduled to appear on the *Today* show on January 27, 1998, to talk about historic preservation. Of course NBC expected her to cancel because she would be in danger of being grilled on the charges against her husband. Stunningly, she didn't. *Today* co-host Matt Lauer was called back from vacation to interview her.

It was another event that allowed the world to see the iron *cojones* of Hillary Rodham Clinton. She got up early at her suite in the Waldorf Astoria, but she didn't seem concerned, though she didn't go in unprepared. While her hair stylist and makeup artist worked to make her look lovely and serene, her aides peppered her with likely questions from Lauer. Everyone knew that though Lauer would present his questions politely, they would be nothing less than a verbal assault on her and Bill that would try to draw Hillary into dramatic admissions, preferably ones that would make ratings-getting news. Lauer's not a bad guy; it's just the way the media works: bad news is always good news.

Shortly before seven, Hillary left the Waldorf by private elevator and got into a limo for the ride to the NBC studios off Sixth Avenue. As the car wove its way through traffic to negotiate the short distance to the NBC building, her assistant Melanie Verver observed Hillary. Hillary was coiffed to perfection, wore a light brown pantsuit, and watched the world go by, Verver thought, with flies figuratively hovering lazily around her head. Verver was later to comment, as stated in Edward Klein's *The Truth About Hillary* that Hillary was, "Not uptight. Not apprehensive" at all.

If she had any idea that the media would not be interested in what she had to say that morning, she was disabused of that notion as her car swung onto 50th Street. There was an army of media there, and the streets were lined with big satellite trucks.

★ ★ ★ ★ ★ ★ ★ ★ ★ ★ ★ ★ ★ ★ ★ ★

Why Hillary Doesn't Always Get Perturbed

Some friends of Hillary Clinton say that one of the reasons that she does not get riled about Bill's adultery sometimes, is that the women he has sex with are clearly no competition. They are low-class and devoid of the kind of intellect and sophistication that she has. What's more, physical beauty is not their strong suit. Gennifer Flowers, Monica Lewinsky, and Paula Jones, for example, all have those characteristics.

But there is another thing that Hillary has to notice. Bill treats the women not as people, but as sex objects. Nowhere is there a more dramatic and sad playing out of this idea than with Monica Lewinsky, who fell head over heels in love with him, and as such would do anything he wanted just so she could be with him. In the end, he discarded her without any regard for her feelings.

★ ★ ★ ★ ★ ★ ★ ★ ★ ★ ★ ★ ★ ★ ★ ★ ★

Hillary was whisked upstairs and greeted by the NBC people, including Jeff Zucker, the producer who must have been doing proverbial back flips at having Hillary for an interview. In the green room, she was given a final powdering and soon was sitting, the picture of decorum, opposite Matt Lauer for all the world to see—and hear.

Lauer immediately launched into the main issue. As he put it:

"There has been one question on the minds of people in this country, Mrs. Clinton, lately. And that is, what is the exact nature of the relationship between your husband and Monica Lewinsky. Has he described the relationship in detail to you?"

"Well," Hillary said, "we've talked at great length. And I think as the matter unfolds, the entire country will have more information . . ."

"You have said, I understand, to some close friends that this is the last great battle. And that one side or the other is going down."

And then Hillary gave what was the most important answer of the interview.

"Well, I don't know if I've been that dramatic. That would sound like a good line from a movie. But I do believe that this is a battle. I mean look at the very people who are involved in this that have popped up in other settings. This is the great story here for anybody who is willing to find it and write about it and explain it, is this vast right-wing conspiracy that has been conspiring against my husband since the incident."

The reference to a conspiracy resonated with a lot of people, though the simple fact is that throughout the interview Hillary was never specific, never gave details who the conspirators were, and why it was a conspiracy. Bottom line: the matador had again evaded the charging media bull. Following her appearance, though there would still be a rough road ahead, Bill clearly started to gather the support of the American people, reflected in his rising poll numbers. By the Spring of 1998, his job rating poll numbers were the highest ever. As Klein says, "Starr was increasingly viewed as a puritanical, sex-obsessed prosecutor." The support of the people, the sense was, had saved Bill . . . and Hillary.

"Former President Clinton's dog, Buddy, got run over recently. Very sad. Hillary said today she feels terrible, because she was aiming at Bill."

—Jay Leno

"Senator Hillary Clinton's brother Tony Rodham was beaten up by a guy who caught him having sex with his girlfriend. Where does that happen? Does that happen anywhere you don't have wheels on your house? ... Today Bill Clinton said he was shocked. He said he didn't know anybody on Hillary's side of the family even had sex."

—Jay Leno

"Bill and I have always loved each other ... I'm proud of my marriage."

—*The Unique Voice of Hillary Rodham Clinton*, 48.

Private eye Ivan Duda said in *Bill & Hillary*: "Her purpose in having me find out about these women was not so she could confront Bill with the hurt attitude ... Instead, it was damage control, pure and simple."

"Clinton has been mulling over titles for his memoirs but publishers have already told him he can't use 'Ass Menagerie.'"

—Craig Kilborn

"Editors are reportedly hoping for a 1,000 page autobiography, but Clinton wants it considerably shorter so it hurts less when Hillary throws it at him."

—Craig Kilborn

"Isn't this amazing? Clinton is getting $8M for his memoir, Hillary got $8M for her memoir. That is $16M for two people who for eight years couldn't remember anything."

—Jay Leno

Who Am I?

In a gripping account punctuated by sobs, the Arkansas woman told *Dateline* that in her hotel room, Bill "turned me around and started kissing me, and that was a real shock. I first pushed him away. I just told him 'no.' . . . He tries to kiss me again. He starts biting on my lip. . . . And then he forced me down on the bed. I just was very frightened. I tried to get away from him. I told him 'no.' . . . He wouldn't listen to me."

My name is Juanita Broaddrick, and I told this to *Dateline NBC* in 1999, twenty-one years after it happened in the Camelot Hotel in Little Rock, Arkansas. My charge was never proved, but neither was it disproved. The man was Bill Clinton, at the time attorney general, the chief law enforcement officer of the state of Arkansas.

> **Jay** **Leno** once flipped through a copy of *Cosmopolitan* magazine, reading a list of sex positions—and adding one of his own: "The Clinton: The man's on top, and the wife's out of town!"

—Funniest Celebrity in Washington contest, C-SPAN, 1999

Hillary Clinton once famously blamed the many scandals which had beset her husband's presidency on a "vast right-wing conspiracy." Some time later, Roger Clinton was arrested for driving under the influence. "Apparently, he was weaving and went off the road up onto somebody's lawn," Jay Leno later explained. "Of course, being a typical Clinton, he blamed the whole thing on a vast right-curb conspiracy."

Q & A

Q: What percentage of people said they would vote against Hillary no matter what?

A: In Spring of 2007, between 39 percent and 50 percent of people.

—*In These Times* by author Susan J. Douglas

Q. What percentage of married women would vote against her?

A. 52 percent of married women, as of Spring 2007—*In These Times*

Dear Abby,

My husband is a liar and a cheat. He has cheated on me from the beginning, and when I confront him he denies everything. What's worse, everyone knows he cheats on me. It is so humiliating. Also, since he lost his job six years ago he hasn't even looked for a new one. All he does is sit around the living room in his underwear and watch TV while I work to pay the bills. Since our daughter went away to college he doesn't even pretend to like me. He keeps calling me a lesbian. What should I do?

—(signed) Clueless

Dear Clueless:

Grow up and dump him. You're a United States Senator from New York now. You don't need him anymore!

"See how liberal I'm becoming!"

—Hillary Clinton in a letter to one of her most
significant mentors, Reverend Donald Jones

CHAPTER 2

From Goldwater to Marx: The Making of Hillary Clinton

★ ★ ★ ★ ★ ★ ★ ★ ★ ★ ★ ★ ★ ★ ★ ★ ★

Hillary," a neighbor named Russ Ambin said, "clearly led an early life that was straight out of a sitcom, á la the *Brady Bunch*." Her father, Hugh, and her mother Dorothy, had moved the family, which included Hillary, three years old, and her two younger brothers, from the mean streets of Chicago to the suburban enclave of Park Ridge. There they settled into a Tudor home on a quiet street lined with elm trees.

Hillary's father, a tough ex-Navy man, was a Conservative Republican, as was his wife and most of the people who lived in the neighborhood. Hillary followed suit.

They lived a quiet existence, were solid Methodist Churchgoers, tended to their house, and supported Republican candidates.

Early on, Hillary started to support Republican political candidates, culminating in her support of presidential candidate Barry Goldwater in 1964 whose book, *Conscience of a Conservative,* she had avidly read. She had gone door to door for him, but of course nothing helped. He was trounced in the national election by Lyndon Johnson.

There is no question, as suggested in Chapter One, that Hillary had driving ambition, inculcated by her parents, particularly her father. It is not too far a leap to say that she spent her entire life—and still does to some extent—trying to please him. And *try* is the operative word here. Hugh Rodham was constantly setting the bar higher and higher, and was not quick to praise. For example, once Hillary came home with a report card that was straight A's. Hugh's comment was that it "must be an easy school."

She was climbing a mountain with no summit.

But one day, when she about fourteen, someone entered her life. Or, as a neighbor from Park Ridge put it, "a fox got into the hen house."

The fox in this case truly came in sheep's clothing. His name was Donald G. Jones and he was hired as the new youth minister. He started to teach, and what he taught had very little to do with books and regular school courses. He began turning students towards what was in the world outside the classroom, and one of his students nicknamed his class "The University of Life."

As Barbara Olson says in *Hell To Pay: The Unfolding Story of Hillary Rodham Clinton*, "Jones possessed an expansive mission to open his students up to his view of the wider world and transform them." Transform them, as it turned out for Hillary, into a whole new way of thinking that motivated her and others to take their first steps on the leftward road.

As Olson said, it seemed Jones's main goal was to "break open the comfortable cocoon of Park Ridge and expose his protégés to the disturbing realities of the contemporary worker."

He did this in a variety of ways—many times shocking.

Once, for example, he brought a man in to argue against the existence of God, and this in a community where almost everyone attended church regularly. Atheists are ordinarily very knowledgeable, if for no other reason than that they have to defend themselves constantly. Jones had to know that many of his young students would not be able to put up an adequate intellectual offense or defense against the man. In other words, his ideas would be imprinted on people who couldn't fight back very well.

Another time, Jones opened up a discussion on teenage pregnancy, a topic that in those days was mostly discussed in shadowy places in hushed voices, if at all. One can assume that this shocked not only the students, including of course Hillary, but the congregation, and lots of people living in nice homes on those quiet elm-tree-lined streets.

But perhaps the most shocking thing of all came when Jones brought the philosophy of Communist Karl Marx into the classroom. It was personified in the theology of Paul Tillich, who Jones believed in absolutely. Tillich redefined Christianity in terms of the German idealistic tradition and existentialism. Jones believed that the major flaw of contemporary Christianity was its deep roots in middle-class culture. Its revival, Tillich argued, could only come from a critique of society that took its inspiration from Marxist lines of thought.

"In this new spin on Christianity," Olson says, "grace, sin, and death and redemption were no longer the key features of theology." The major problem facing American youth, Jones said, was a crisis of meaning and alienation. They were the kids that J.D. Salinger epitomized in *Catcher in the Rye*.

To understand this better, Jones took the impressionable young people on various field trips not to the zoo or the museum, or to see the Cubs or the White Sox play, but into the bowels, the slums, of Chicago, where they viewed how the other half lived. Jones threw poverty and hopelessness in their teenage faces, and reinforced it with his narration. They listened, they felt, and shouldered guilt that that would last a lifetime.

Years later Jones said to Arkansas journalist Meredith Oakley, "I don't think those kids had ever seen poverty before. Religion, going to church, tended to function there for most people to reinforce their traditional conservative values, and so when I came in and took that white, middle class youth group into the inner city of Chicago, that was quite radical." In other words, what he taught them went beyond mere compassion; he inculcated them with a philosophy that was decidedly pink in color.

When Jones left the ministry two years after he had arrived for another teaching job at Drew University in New Jersey, as Barbara Olson reports in *Hell To Pay*, many of his congregants, in a sense, waved goodbye happily.

"The unfettered free market has been the most radically disruptive force in American life in the last generation."

—Hillary Clinton

"We're all going to have to rethink how we deal with the Internet. As exciting as these new developments are, there are a number of serious issues without any kind of editing function or gatekeeping function."

—First Lady Hillary Clinton, in 1998, days after the Monica Lewinsky story was reported on the *Drudge Report*

"We're saying that for America
to get back on track, we're going to cut [the Bush
tax cuts] short and not give it to you. We're going to
take things away from you on behalf
of the common good."

—Hillary Clinton, in a 2004 fundraising
speech to wealthy liberals in San Francisco

But the die was indeed cast for Hillary Rodham. Though she was crestfallen when Goldwater lost the election, Hillary no longer took much stock in the precepts he detailed in *Conscience of a Conservative*. As Olson says, "She found herself thinking more in terms of mass social action, of a Christian socialism where the restraints of Christianity gradually gave way to the demands of politics and power." In other words, anything went, as long as your goals were achieved. Indeed, today both Clintons adhere to whatever is necessary to achieve their goals, such as hiring private eyes, dirt diggers and apologists to win the day.

The man who taught her this anything-goes methodology was Saul Alinsky, a heavyset Chicagoan. Don Jones introduced her to Alinsky, and if Jones did the groundwork in terms of socialistic impulses, Alinsky added the rest. His radical political philosophy helped change her forever.

Alinsky himself was a radical of the firebrand type. Born in 1909, in his heyday in the '30s he focused his energy on helping impoverished groups, such as the people who lived around the stockyards in Chicago where he was born. The meatpackers, Alinsky said with a slight smile, announced him a "subversive menace." But of course he liked that, and was particularly appreciative of the *Chicago Tribune*. "Their adoption of me as a public enemy of law and order, a radical's radical, gave me a perennial and constantly renewable baptismal certificate in the city of Chicago." He was born again, alright—a born again nightmare.

Alinsky and his supporters grew and spread in the '40s and as Barbara Olson says "Took it as a matter of pride that he was arrested frequently and touted that he was under FBI surveillance."

Then in 1947 Alinsky came out with an explosive book called *Reveille for Radicals*, which was a bestseller. In it, he argues against trying to reform capitalism, but advocates a direct takeover of power. Then, in 1971, he published *Rules for Radicals*, and people involved in social protest had found their prophet.

To properly understand Hillary—and understanding is highly significant in stopping her—one must grasp that at the heart of Alinsky's way is deviousness and *winning any way you can*. Indeed, deviousness and duplicity are very much allowed as long as it produced the desired result. Hillary, today a mistress of deceit, incorporated the ideas into her methods.

To Alinsky, and later to Clinton, the goal was accumulating power. To do this, as he said, one must "win the trust of one's charges" any way one can, and leaders just have to keep that in mind: Do whatever has to be done to get those people behind them and keep the people there.

Alinsky had no regard for leaders who turned off and ultimately turned away followers. One of the best examples of this was the volatile group of the 1960s—SDS, or Students for a Democratic Society. In no uncertain terms Alinsky counseled them to change the way they dressed, dampen their rhetoric and language, not be ashamed of their middle-class roots. As he said in *Rules for Radicals*:

> Our rebels have contemptuously rejected the values and ways of the life of the middle class . . . They have stigmatized it as a materialistic, decadent bourgeois, degenerate, imperialistic, war mongering, brutalized and corrupt. They are right, but we must begin from where we are if we are to build power for change, and the power and the people are in the big middle-class majority. Therefore it is useless self-indulgence for an activist to put his past behind him. Instead, he should realize the priceless value of the middle-class experience. His middle-class identity, his familiarity with the values and problems, are invaluable for organization of his own people.

He will know that a 'square' should not be dismissed as such, instead his own approach must be, 'square enough to get the action started.'

Alinsky was well aware that America was the kind of country where one could rebel: "True, there is government harassment, but there still is that relative freedom to fight. I can attack my government, try to organize or change it. That's more than I can do in Moscow, Peking, or Havana . . . Parts of the far left have gone so far in the political circle that they are now all but indistinguishable from the extreme right."

Hillary stayed in contact with Alinsky through her college days at Wellesley in Connecticut. He was so impressed with her that he wanted her to get an internship to study with him. Instead, she went on to Yale Law School. But her change in thinking was well developed before she met Alinsky, thanks to her exposure to Don Jones. Gradually, Hillary had found herself identifying more and more with liberal causes. Her transformation seemed to be complete when she learned that John Lindsay, a tall, handsome man who has was decidedly liberal, had been elected mayor of New York City. Though still a Republican, she admitted in a letter to Jones how happy she was with the election's outcome, and said she was leaning left. "See how liberal I'm becoming!"

This was electrifyingly obvious when she delivered the commencement address at Wellesley College in Connecticut to resounding applause, a performance that was to put her on the cover of *Life* magazine, perhaps the most important magazine of its time.

The Wellesley audience was ready for the speech. In the late 1960s, Wellesley was a hotbed of liberalism. Students discussed such topics as government, politics, civil rights, and civil liberties with fire in their eyes.

For Hillary, more social activism went hand in hand with this, which included teaching poor black children in Roxbury, Massachusetts how to read, becoming active in Vietnam war student protests, and increasingly vocal in her opposition to anything conservative and backed by the government.

Hillary mourned tearfully when Martin Luther King, Jr. was assassinated, but the single event that drove out her residue of Republicanism was Bobby Kennedy's assassination. Though a member of the campus Young Republicans, she withdrew . . . and traveled as far to the left as she could in American politics, openly supporting Eugene McCarthy's quest for presidential nomination. But when he dropped out, rather than support the Republican candidate, Richard Nixon, she supported his opponent, Hubert Humphrey, who looked like he was going to win the election.

As time went by, her liberalism made its way into the marrow of her political bones. She had become a force to be reckoned with on campus; in her senior year,1969, she was chosen to give the commencement address. It was a time when America was embroiled in the Vietnam War, Civil Rights, and a host of other disquieting events. Senator Edward Brooke, a liberal Republican from Massachusetts, gave a sort of standard commencement address.

The speech Hillary was to make had been shown to and approved by the president of Wellesley, but as the latter was to ruefully learn, even though she extracted a promise from Hillary that she would not deviate from the prepared and approved text, Hillary would deviate—and then some.

First Brooke, who supported President Nixon, spoke. He touched on poverty, Civil Rights, and Vietnam, but he criticized the role of small groups, such as the SDS (Students for a Democratic Society), and harped on violence as not being a means to accomplishing anything.

Brooke missed the point, missed the fiery emotions that were boiling inside his audience. They wanted results now, not hopeful platitudes, and by whatever means they could be obtained. They wanted people to be free, the war to end, and the bastards who were profiting from it all driven into a hole in the ground and then covered with dirt.

Hillary, of course, was one of those raging when she stood up to speak at the completion of Brooke's speech. She also wanted to change the future but, as one of her fellow students put it, "starting last Thursday." And contrary to her having given her word to the president of the college, when she spoke off the cuff she, as Barbara Olson put it, "extinguished all hopes that charity, generosity, respect, and good manners might reign that day."

Surprise, then shock, rippled through the audience as Hillary ripped into a United States Senator, a Civil Rights icon, an African American man before a liberal audience and characterized him as a "craven apologist," Hillary made some good points, but Olson characterized much of the speech as having "undertones of German Existential philosophy, '60s psychobabble and part youthful, egocentric angst." Olson said that if someone today presented such a "convoluted stew "as Hillary did in that speech, it "would be seen not as a courageous declaration of identity, but as a hopeless meandering of feminist platitudes and catch sound bites that would cause listeners to look away out of embarrassment for the speaker. As a style it could be called first person, subjective." But it made Hillary famous—or infamous.

Another indication of how radical she had become related to her college thesis, which claimed that people in poverty should have a greater say in how help is given to them. It was read by her professors then, but no one can read it today. When her husband became president, Wellesley instituted a rule that no one in public life would have their college work exposed. One gets the sense that it was the Clintons who were responsible for the rule. They would not relish the idea today of her leftward thinking being exposed.

★ ★ ★ ★ ★ ★ ★ ★ ★ ★ ★ ★ ★ ★ ★ ★

Key Alinsky Tactics, Including Assault by Fart

Saul Alinsky taught a number of things to his followers. Among the key tactics were:

1. *Power is not only what you have but what the enemy thinks you have.* For example, if you go into an area with one hand in your pocket and start giving hints that you are holding a gun, people will give you wide berth, even though you may be just gripping your car keys.

2. *Never go outside the experience of your people.* So if, for example, your followers were longshoremen with no familiarity with college campus life, he would not advocate putting them in that situation.

3. *Whenever possible, go outside the experience of the enemy.* For this precept, Alinsky cited the "Sherman's March to the Sea," where instead of keeping a conduit open between his army and supply depot, Sherman lived off the land and the plantations he grabbed.

4. *Make the enemy live up to their own rule book. You can kill them with this, for they can no more live up to their own rules than the Christian church can live up to Christianity.* In her book, Barbara Olson said, "Alinsky excelled at forcing his opponents to violate their own standards and then forcing them to capitulate out of shame.

5. *Ridicule is man's most potent weapon.* Alinsky felt that ridicule hobbled one's enemies like no other action, and he sometimes advocated carrying ridicule to great

lengths. He once suggested, as Barbara Olson says in her book, buying a hundred tickets to the Rochester symphony and giving them to the first one hundred black people who responded to an offer of a free dinner of baked beans. "The establishment," Alinsky wrote, would not in its wildest fears "expect an attack on their prize cultural jewel, their fame symphony orchestra. Regular stink bombs are illegal and cause for immediate arrest, but there would be absolutely nothing here that the police department or the ushers or any other servants could do about it. The law would be completely paralyzed."

While the idea bordered on ludicrous, it was typical of the kinds of legal sabotage Alinsky could create, acts employed to reduce people to powerlessness. The tactic also satisfied other Alinsky precepts, like going outside the experience of the enemy.

But no doubt the biggest Alinsky tactic used by Hillary Clinton—and Bill—over the years, in addition to the army of dirt diggers, private eyes, and apologists they used over the years, is what Alinsky characterized as "mass jujitsu," where one let the enemy move first and then use his own momentum against him.

Alinsky also advocated straightforward attack. As he said, "Pick the target, freeze it, personalize it, and polarize it."

★ ★ ★ ★ ★ ★ ★ ★ ★ ★ ★ ★ ★ ★ ★ ★

The road leftward continued at Yale, the degree shown by her involvement with the Black Panthers. She had a law professor named Emerson, nicknamed "Tommie the Commie," and it was through him that Hillary was introduced to lawyer Charles Garry who regularly defended the Panthers, and who helped her gain access to the group.

At the time—1970—one of the violent leaders of the group, Bobby Seale, was being tried in New Haven for the torture and murder of another Black Panther named Alex Rackley, who the Panthers thought was a confidential informant for the police. There were three Panthers involved, and two of them copped a plea. Only Bobby Seale, who had been in California, resisted extradition and became, to Hillary and other protesters, a cause to rally around the Black Panthers against the repressive white establishment.

Like all of these groups, Hillary and others engaged in selective or pigeonhole thinking, which included not even determining if the Panthers were guilty of murder. It was just a great cause to gather around and whoop about. Small wonder. In fact, though, the evidence against the Panthers was overwhelming, and included part of an audio tape where Rackley was tried for the crime of betrayal.

As a massive May strike in support of Seale was to occur on the University campus, Yale president Kingman

Brewster capitulated by issuing a statement which was sympathetic not only to the students but to the Black Panthers, and even allowed Charles Garry to make his residence on campus. It was a complete and utter sellout.

For her part, Hillary did not utter any protests despite the violent rhetoric of Panthers and their supporters including calling for police assassinations and such phrases as "If Bobby dies, Yale fries." Indeed as Barbara Olson says: "As part of her coursework for Professor Emerson, Hillary attended the Black Panther trials and put her considerable leadership and organization skills to work by organizing shifts of fellow students to monitor the trial and report alleged civil rights abuses."

Ultimately, the New Haven jury was hung on a verdict, but shortly thereafter Seale was sent to jail for four years for inciting a riot in Chicago in the wake of the Democratic Convention. The Black Panthers eventually disintegrated, and there are few observers today who would describe it as anything but a violent, militant group whose purpose, more than justice, was to hurt.

It's really astonishing that Hillary could support such a group, and even if it didn't say anything about her political leanings—which of course it does—it says volumes about her lack of judgment.

Even Then They Didn't Like Her

When Hillary was in high school, says Barbara Olson in *Hell to Pay: The Unfolding Story of Hillary Rodham Clinton*, there were signs that even though she was a Republican then rather than a Democrat she was "respected but not terribly well liked." "Southwards revealingly predicted that she would become a nun—Sister Frigidaire." Another Southwards item with a crude drawing of Hillary is headlined "Lawyer Hillary Reviews Career."

★ ★ ★ ★ ★ ★ ★ ★ ★ ★ ★ ★ ★ ★ ★ ★

Who Said That?

1) "We're going to take things away from you on behalf of the common good."

   A. Karl Marx

   B. Adolph Hitler

   C. Joseph Stalin

   D. None of the above

2) "It's time for a new beginning, for an end to government of the few, by the few, and for the few . . . And to replace it with shared responsibility for shared prosperity."

   A. Lenin

   B. Mussolini

C. Idi Amin

D. None of the above

3) "(We) . . . can't just let business as usual go on, and that means something has to be taken away from some people."

A. Nikita Khruschev

B. Josef Goebbels

C. Boris Yeltsin

D. None of the above

4) "We have to build a political consensus and that requires people to give up a little bit of their own . . . in order to create this common ground."

A. Mao Tse Tung

B. Hugo Chavez

C. Kim Jong II

D. None of the above

5) "I certainly think the free-market has failed."

A. Karl Marx

B. Lenin

C. Molotov

D. None of the above

6) "I think it's time to send a clear message to what has become the most profitable sector in (the) entire economy that they are being watched."

A. Pinochet

B. Milosevic

C. Saddam Hussein

D. None of the above.

"We just can't trust the American people to make these types of decisions. ...Government has to make these choices for people."

—Hillary Clinton, circa 1993, speaking to Rep. Dennis Hastert on the issue of who should control the allocation of money in her healthcare reform plan

Answers

(1) D. None of the above. Statement was made by Hillary Clinton 6/29/2004

(2) D. None of the above. Statement was made by Hillary Clinton 5/29/2007

(3) D. None of the above. Statement was made by Hillary Clinton 6/4/2007

(4) D. None of the above. Statement was made by Hillary
Clinton 6/4/2007
(5) D. None of the above. Statement was made by Hillary
Clinton 6/4/2007
(6) D. None of the above. Statement was made by Hillary
Clinton 9/2/2005

–Source: Common Internet Posting, source unknown

★ ★ ★ ★ ★ ★ ★ ★ ★ ★ ★ ★ ★ ★ ★ ★

"We can't afford to have that money go to the private sector. The money has to go to the federal government because the federal government will spend that money better than the private sector will spend it."

—Hillary Clinton, in 1993,
regarding healthcare reform

★ ★ ★ ★ ★ ★ ★ ★ ★ ★ ★ ★ ★ ★ ★ ★

More Rules for Radicals by Alinsky

• "Life is a corrupting process from the time a child
learns to play his mother off against his father in the

politics of when to go to bed; he who fears corruption, fears life."

- "It is not enough to persuade them of your competence, talents, and courage—they must have faith in your ability and courage. They must believe in your capacity not just to provide the opportunity for action, power, change, adventure, a piece of the drama of life, but to give them a very definite promise, almost an assurance of victory."

- "It is useless self-indulgence for an activist to put his past behind him. Instead, he should realize the priceless value of his middle-class experience. His middle-class identity, his familiarity with the values and problems, are invaluable for organization of his 'own people.'"

- "What was my alternative? To draw myself up into righteous moral indignation, saying, I would rather lose than corrupt my principles, and then go home with my ethical hymen intact?"

- "The human spirit glows from that small inner light of doubt whether we are right, while those who believe with complete certainty that they possess the right are dark inside and darken the world outside with cruelty, pain, and injustice. Those who enshrine the poor or have-nots are as guilty as other dogmatists and just as dangerous."

- "Ethical standards must be elastic to stretch with the times."

- "Let nothing get you off your target."

- "Effective organization is thwarted by the desire for instant and dramatic change, or as I have phrased it elsewhere, the demand for revelation rather than revolution."
- "He knows that all values are relative, in a world of political relativity."
- "One's concern with the ethics of means and ends varies inversely with one's profound interest in the issue."
- "Power is the very essence, the dynamo of life. It is the power of the heart pumping blood and sustaining life in the body."

Source: *Hell To Pay*, Barbara Olson

CHAPTER 3

Lies and BS

★ ★ ★ ★ ★ ★ ★ ★ ★ ★ ★ ★ ★ ★ ★ ★ ★

> "She's duplicitous. She would say or do anything that would forward her ambitions. She can look you straight in the eye and lie, and sort of not know she's lying."

—Liz Moynihan, wife of Pat Moynihan,
the esteemed senator from New York State

If Hillary instead of George Washington were asked if she chopped down the cherry tree, she might have said something like "It depends on what your definition of a cherry tree is . . ."

Hillary is known for double, triple and quadruple speak and outright lying. This chapter contains a lineup of more of her bold-faced lies and smarmy but many times skillful ways to avoid flat out lying.

She lied or bent the truth on a number of serious issues, and ones not so serious as well. One serious issue was Iraq; Hillary was caught with her famous pantsuit down. These days, as she runs for president, she is desperately trying to back away from her vote authorizing the war. But in an article written by Don van Netta and Jeff Gerth in the *New York Times* called "Hillary's War" she did indeed vote for it and since then has tried to back off from her vote, and has resisted pressure from the Democratic Party powers to at least apologize for it. Indeed, as she talks to voters she accents her reservations about voting for the war more than anything else.

She seems to have a real problem, Van Netta and Gerth said, with saying "I screwed up." Her story now is that she voted for the war, but it's really not her fault that she did, and that George Bush lied to her. She said she actually though that more inspectors were going to continue to search for WMDs. As she says: "What I did not count on . . . is that he [Bush] had no intention to allow the inspectors to finish the job."

Now, as Gerth and Van Netta also point out, writer Tom Kuiper says the war resolution contained no directive for further U.N. inspections in Iraq. It was left to the president to see if his approach was working, to determine Saddam Hussein's compliance, and invade if necessary.

Sen. Carl Levin offered an amendment that would have required additional U.N. action and if that failed, the President, Kuiper says, would have had to return to Congress to get authorization to go to war. But Hillary, who now claims that more diplomacy was key, voted against this. Said the article: "Clinton has never publicly explained her vote against the Levin amendment or said why she stayed on the sidelines as eleven other senators debated it for ninety-five minutes that day."

Van Netta and Gerth said that the day before Sen. Clinton voted for the war resolution, she spoke on the floor of the Senate and talked about "intelligence reports" describing Saddam's rebuilding his WMD stock and about Saddam giving "aid, comfort, and sanctuary to terrorists, including al-Qaeda members."

Bill Clinton was, according to the reporters, her chief advisor on the war vote. They quote him saying at the time, "Mark my words, he will develop weapons of mass destruction . . . He will deploy them and he will use them."

She was still pro war after returning from a trip to Iraq in 2003. She spoke at the Council on Foreign Relations in New York about the situation, and seemed ready to go to war. "We have no option but to stay involved and committed," she said, calling her vote "the right vote" and one "I stand by."

She also appeared on *Meet the Press* during a 2005 trip to Iraq and, again, according to Gerth and Van Netta, continued to express confidence in the effort and opposed withdrawal or a timetable. "We don't want to send a signal to insurgents, to the terrorists, that we are going to be out of here at some, you know, date certain."

The issue here is not making mistakes, says Tom Kuiper, it is being honest and taking responsibility. Says Kuiper: "It is simply nauseating to hear from someone who aspires to be president of the United States what we heard from Clinton at the New Hampshire debate: '. . . this is George Bush's war . . . He started the war. He mismanaged the war. He is responsible for the war.' But there would have been no Iraq invasion without authorization from Congress. Clinton's vote was part of that authorization. It was her war as it was George Bush's war."

A number of other lies are not significant in terms of the portrait they paint of the liar. One was about Hillary's daughter Chelsea, who she said in her autobiography *Living History* was in danger on 9/11 because she had been jogging in the area of the Twin Towers, and actually witnessed the impact of the planes against the buildings. Meanwhile the person who debunked the story was Chelsea herself. In a magazine article she said that she was nowhere near the towers when the planes hit, and in fact was asleep in a room on the other side of the city and was awakened by a phone call and told about the event. She spent the rest of the day watching the tragedy unfold on TV. So Hillary took a tremendous tragedy and tried to make political hay out of it.

Embarrassing Moment

Shortly after the publication of *Living History* (her memoirs) in 2003, Hillary Clinton attended a press conference in New York. She took a few questions from the press . . . and then began to work the crowd. People kept asking her to pose for pictures or to sign things—mostly copies of *Living History*, but also baseballs, brochures from the fair, and scraps of used paper and envelopes. One man handed her a copy of *Time* magazine with a menacing-looking picture of her on the cover and the headline "The Truth About Whitewater." Clinton looked nonplussed, but signed it anyway.

Source: Anectodotage.com

Another lie in the book was perhaps the stupidest she ever told because it was so easy to debunk. In this, one day she met world famous mountain climber Sir Edmund Hillary—the first person to scale Mount Everest—at Katmandu Airport. She instantly launched into a scenario that was pure BS, telling reporters her mother named her after Sir Edmund. To make the lie more believable, she fattened it with persuasive details like her mother had read an article about Sir Edmund when she was pregnant, and admired him. "So when I was born," Hillary said, "she called me Hillary and she always told me it's because of Sir Edmund Hillary."

Later, reporters learned that since Clinton was born in 1947 the story didn't fly because the other Hillary climbed Mount Everest on May 29, 1953—almost six years after Hillary was born.

Sometimes her lies are more doublespeak, more involved BS answers than straightforward lies—and some astute critics have caught her. In pointed political broadsides from some of the major liberal-leaning publications—including the *New York Times* and the *Washington Post*—Senator Clinton has been the target of surprisingly sharp criticism about her refusal to answer policy questions, investigative reporting about her husband's business dealings and unsavory fund raisers, and even assertions that her candidacy was solely beholden to her husband's political influence.

For instance, when asked by NBC's Tim Russert in a Democratic presidential debate about whether following in her husband's presidential footsteps was creating a dynasty, Mrs. Clinton said, "I'm running on my own. I'm going to the people on my own." But that answer didn't wash with Maureen Dowd, the columnist for the *New York Times*. "Without nepotism, Hillary would be running for the president of Vassar," she said in her column. "Of course, Hillary is never on her own. From the beginning, her campaign has relied on her husband's donors, network, strategies and strong-arming."

Other columnists and reporters similarly piled on Mrs. Clinton in the aftermath of the Dartmouth College debate that was seen by them as a litany of evasive answers. In a post-debate analysis of Mrs. Clinton's "evasiveness on issues," such as troop withdrawals in Iraq, saving Social Security, and whether Israel has the right to attack Iran, Associated Press writer Beth Fouhy said she "adopted the time-honored, front-runner strategy of dodging tough questions, contradicting the image of a strong leader. Examples of Clinton's evasiveness were manifest Wednesday night."

When Mr. Russert asked how she intended to save Social Security from future insolvency and whether higher payroll taxes would be on the negotiating table, Mrs. Clinton refused to say what options she would propose, saying she first wanted to "move toward fiscal responsibility." Writing in the *New York Times*, columnist Gail Collins said, "This is an excellent example of how to string together the maximum number of weasel words in one sentence. It was also pretty typical of Hillary's entire evening."

In a 1,558 word piece in the *Times* on Sunday, titled "Is Hillary Clinton the New Old Al Gore?" after her TV appearances to defend her healthcare reform plan, Frank Rich said, "she seemed especially evasive when dealing with questions requiring human reflection instead of wonkery."

A Vow Broken

Hillary vowed—on the grave of old friend Vince Foster—that she would never run for President, and that she would never run for senator either.

—Tom Kuiper

★ ★ ★ ★ ★ ★ ★ ★ ★ ★ ★ ★ ★ ★ ★ ★

The Clinton Cackle

When Hillary doesn't want to answer a question, she often issues an empty laugh which has come to be known as the "Clinton Cackle." There is a range of YouTube videos splicing together clips of the slightly mirthless laugh that she sometimes uses to deflect awkward questions. This shows her face morphing into that of the Wicked Witch of the East from *The Wizard of Oz*. But essentially she doesn't answer the question.

★ ★ ★ ★ ★ ★ ★ ★ ★ ★ ★ ★ ★ ★ ★ ★

Questioner to Hillary Clinton: What's your name?

Hillary: First or last?

Questioner: Both.

Hillary: You mean what it was before I was married?

Questioner:	Yes.
Hillary:	I had two names.
Question:	What do you mean?
Hillary:	Just what I said.
Question:	What did you say?
Hillary:	You don't know? You're the one asking the questions?
Questioner:	I am, but I'm not getting any answers.
Hillary:	Just take a deep breath, focus and ask the question slowly and clearly.
Questioner:	Ah, fuck it.
Hillary:	Fuck who?
Questioner:	Fuck you.
Hillary:	I'd surely like that. It hasn't happened in a long, long time.

Hillary's 2003 mega bestseller *Living History* is notable for not telling the truth, or the complete truth, about a variety of her experiences. A good example of this is an event that occurred with the Black Panthers. She writes in the book, "The world and its realities came crashing down on Yale in April 1970, when eight Black Panthers, including party leader Bobby Seale, were put on trial for murder in New Haven. Thousands of angry protesters, convinced the Panthers had been set up by the FBI and government prosecutors, swarmed into the city. Demonstrations broke out in and around campus. The campus was bracing for a huge May Day rally to support the Panthers when I learned, late on the night of April 27, that the International Law Library, which was in the basement of the law school, was on fire. Horrified, I rushed to join a bucket brigade of faculty, staff, and students to put out the fire and to rescue books damaged by flames and water."

Here, Hillary makes it seem as if that was her only involvement was as a firefighter. But as reported by Kincaid, it was a bit more than that. Former '60s radical David Horowitz , the report says, says that both "Hillary Rodham and Bill Lann Lee, who later became President Clinton's head of the U.S. Justice Department's Civil Rights Division, helped organize the pro-Panther demonstrations at Yale. Others sympathetic to Hillary contend that she was merely among a group of law students who monitored the trial on behalf of the ACLU, which was concerned that law enforcement was violating the civil liberties of members of the party. But Hillary says nothing in her book about this role."

"What is not in dispute," Kincaid says, "is that she served on the Board of Editors of the *Yale Review of Law and Social Action*, a 'progressive' alternative to the school's traditional review, and that its fall 1970 issue was devoted to the trial and glorifying the Panthers."

Another area where there is a problem with the truth is her involvement with a Communistic-tinged law firm in the summer of 1971. She says she was a law clerk at the

Oakland, California, firm of Treuhaft, Walker and Burnstein. "I spent most of my time working for Mal Burnstein researching, writing legal motions and briefs for a child custody case," she said.

Not quite, Kincaid says. Public record shows that "Clinton worked for Robert Treuhaft, a member of the Communist Party USA (CPUSA) and Harvard-trained lawyer for the party." Backing this up was author Peter Flaherty in his book, *The First Lady* (Vital Issues Press, 1996). He says that "Hillary was recommended to Treuhaft by some of her professors at Yale. She was looking for a 'movement' law firm to work at for the summer. As it turns out, Hillary would continue her association and support of the Black Panther cause while working as a law clerk for Treuhaft." Treuhaft told Herb Caen of the *San Francisco Examiner*, "that was the time we were representing the Black Panthers, and she worked on that case."

Mrs. Clinton's involvement with Treuhaft is no secret, although Hillary clearly doesn't want to talk about it. A *New York Times* obituary of Treuhaft, who died in 2001, said that he had "accepted a young Yale lawyer named Hillary Rodham as an intern." A British newspaper, the *London Times*, said that "generations of liberal lawyers were groomed under his [Treuhaft's] tutelage, including a young Yale law student named Hillary Rodham."

These two obituaries are posted at a website in honor of Treuhaft's famous wife, British author Jessica Mitford, herself a Communist and member of the CPUSA whose lobbying of Bill Clinton on the death penalty issue was reportedly facilitated by Hillary.

The Harvard Law Bulletin said about Treuhaft, "He belonged to and served as attorney to the Communist Party of the United States for many years and defended the civil rights of groups such as the Black Panther Party, Vietnam War draft resisters, and members of Berkeley's free speech movement."

Despite her Communist connection, "Hillary," said Barbara Olson, "has never repudiated (involvement) with the Communist movement in America or explained her relationship with two of its leading adherents. Of course, no one has pursued these questions with Hillary. She has shown she will not answer hard questions about her past, and she has learned that she does not need to—remarkable in an age when political figures are allowed such little privacy."

In her own book, however, Hillary does write about some of her radical associates. She notes a meeting in 1969 with David Mixner of the Vietnam Moratorium Committee, an anti-Vietnam war protest group that came under investigation by the House Internal Security Subcommittee for its involvement with Communists and backing from Hanoi. Mixner would go on to become a leading homosexual activist, adviser to and friend of President Clinton. He was credited with delivering some six million votes to Clinton in 1992.

David Brock's book, *The Seduction of Hillary Rodham*, links Hillary with Robert Borosage, a Yale Law School graduate and one of the founders of the *Yale Review*, who would later become director of the Institute for Policy Studies (IPS), a Marxist think tank. Borosage is now co-director of the Campaign for America's Future, a group trying to move the Democratic Party further to the political left.

Hillary writes about her involvement with the Children's Defense Fund, headed by Marian Wright Edelman, as Cliff Kincaid, writer and editor for AIM, Accuracy in Media, reports but omits any mention of the New World Foundation (NWF). Hillary followed Edelman's husband, Peter, as chairman of the NWF. Mrs. Clinton chaired the group during a time, 1982–1988, when it gave grants to the Committee in Solidarity with the People of El Salvador, a front group for the communist terrorists; the National Lawyers Guild, a one-time-identified communist front; and the Christic Institute, an extreme left-wing group of lawyers which practiced "legal terrorism" against citizens, retired military and intelligence officials, and others who were perceived to be supporting the cause of freedom from communism in Central America.

But Kincaid says Peter Flaherty writes, "Hillary's official biography, prepared by the '92 Clinton campaign, makes no mention of her stint as NWF chairman, despite the fact that she oversaw some $23 million in foundation assets. A few journalists, like Dan Wattenberg of the *American Spectator*, did report on the NWF grants during the summer of 1992, but the major media paid almost no attention. There was no need for Hillary to defend herself."

Hillary, Kincaid says, also took advantage of Bill Clinton's radical connections, many developed in his trips abroad. Strobe Talbott and Bill Clinton had been Rhodes Scholars in England together, for example, and Talbott and his wife, Brooke Shearer, "became friends of mine," she writes. Brooke's brother, Derek Shearer, another Yale graduate, became a friend of Bill and pro-Marxist economic adviser to Clinton.

Talbott, who also graduated from Yale and is now president of the Brookings Institution, became deputy secretary of state in the Clinton administration. Before that, he had been a columnist for *Time* magazine, writing in a July 20, 1992, column, "The Birth of the Global Nation," that in the next century "nationhood as we know it will be obsolete," that we would all some day become world citizens, and that wars and human rights violations in the twentieth century had clinched "the case for world government."

To help accomplish this, Talbott pressed for the use of the U.S. military to restore an extreme leftist, defrocked Catholic priest, Jean Bertrand Aristide, to power in Haiti in 1994. Confidential documents from the U.N., publicized by AIM at the time, said that Talbott and other officials viewed an invasion as "politically desirable."

Kincaid says that Aristide, a Marxist-oriented advocate of Liberation Theology, had been booted from the presidency by the military because, among other things, he was inciting mobs to threaten to burn to death judges and legislators if they did not do his bidding.

Hillary's book describes this as a case of "the elected president" of Haiti being returned to power "after a harrowing year of diplomacy and the landing of American troops." But the book, *Voodoo Politics* by Lynn Garrison, tells a far different story, exposing Aristide as an anti-American figure not only allegedly involved in murder but drug trafficking. Garrison was an adviser to one of the generals involved in the anti-Aristide coup. The political reasons for the invasion can be seen in the makeup of the Aristide Foundation for Democracy, whose board included left-wing Democrats such as Reps. Maxine Waters, John Conyers, and Joseph Kennedy, and former Rep. Michael Barnes.

Talbott's global left-wing vision was endorsed by President Clinton, who had sent a June 22, 1993, letter to the World Federalist Association (WFA) when it gave Talbott its Norman Cousins Global Governance Award. In the letter, Clinton noted that Norman Cousins, the WFA founder, had "worked for world peace and world government" and that Talbott was a "worthy recipient" of the award.

Hillary won't publicly discuss communist Chinese financial contributions to her husband's campaign for re-election, but she admits that the communist dictatorship wanted to use her appearance at a 1995 U.N. women's conference in Beijing as "a public relations tool to improve its image around the world." Hillary went anyway. She doesn't mention that radical feminist and Marxist Bella Abzug played a role in getting her to go. Hillary was a big fan of

Abzug, having hailed her work and career in a major speech at the U.N.

FBI files identify Abzug as a member of the CPUSA. She ran for Congress but was opposed by the Socialist Party for having shown "a general unwillingness to be outspokenly critical of Communist actions threatening the peace and freedom of the world."

Not too far from the five-star hotel where Hillary and the feminists were meeting in Beijing, baby girls and boys were being starved to death in Chinese orphanages.

Pictures of this brutality were smuggled out of the country by Human Rights Watch. One showed an emaciated eleven-year-old girl tied down to a bed, withering away to nothing. A British film about the problem, *The Dying Rooms*, showed children tied to wooden toilets, sleeping in their own excrement.

The brutality reflects the Chinese policy of one child per family, enforced through mandatory abortions, sterilization, and outright killings. Hillary calls such a policy "barbaric" in her book but admits that in her speech to the conference she did not criticize China by name. Ironically, all of this is recounted in a chapter entitled "Women's Rights Are Human Rights."

For Hillary, the villains, says Kincaid, are not the Communists and fellow travelers but the "extreme conservatives" who oppose them. She rails against conservative talk-radio, suggesting that it played a role in provoking the 1994 Oklahoma bombing.

Mrs. Clinton, who abandoned her pro-Palestinian stance and became pro-Israel when she ran for the Senate, speaks out on foreign policy, confirming the role of co-president she assumed in domestic and foreign affairs. Her book defends the Clinton administration's military campaigns on behalf of the Muslims in Bosnia and Kosovo. She says the Bosnian Serbs were attacked, Kincaid reports, because they "were besieging the Muslim town of Srebrenica in a frenzy of 'ethnic cleansing'." In fact, Srebrenica, a so-called U.N. "safe haven," was being used to train and refurbish Muslim troops, and may have been serving as a base for foreign terrorists in the region. Hillary conveniently ignores the Clinton-approved "ethnic cleansing" by Croatian forces against the Serbs.

"I had spoken out strongly in favor of Bill's leadership of NATO in the bombing campaign to force Slobodan Milosevic's troops out of Kosovo," she says. But the House refused to authorize the bombing, making the intervention illegal. The bombing campaign, which resulted in the deaths of thousands of innocent civilians, amounted to interference in a sovereign state that posed no threat to the U.S. Indeed, the bombing benefited the Kosovo Liberation Army, a group linked to al Qaeda. In Hillary's book, though, President Clinton "sounded the alarm on global terrorism" and tried to get the "diabolical" Osama bin Laden.

In Rwanda, she writes, "rape and sexual assault were committed on a mass scale, tactical weapons in the genocidal violence that raged there in 1994." Yet she also notes that Bill later "publicly expressed regret that our country and the international community had not done more to stop the horror" of perhaps one million dead. The program *Triumph of Evil* noted that the Clinton administration even hesitated to label it genocide.

But anyone looking at her record can easily find more lies, half truths, and self-serving silences.

Dick Morris, a former Clinton political adviser, said that Hillary, lured by the drop in Bush's ratings, would seek and might win the Democratic nomination this year. Her background will be a problem for her, but even more damaging are the lies she has told about her close friend, Webb Hubbell, who went to prison for stealing from his partners and clients of the Rose law firm.

Hillary writes in her book that she didn't know Webb Hubbell, an old friend and partner from her law firm days, was in serious trouble until November 24, 1994. That is a lie. She and Bill had been told in March that Hubbell faced prosecution and that he should be ousted from the Justice Department. They promptly sought and got his resignation. Fearing he would reveal their darkest secrets, Kincaid says, they and their aides set out to raise money to buy his silence. The final OIC report says he was paid $541,750, ostensibly for his services, but he performed little or no work.

The claim that the Clintons didn't know Hubbell was in deep trouble until November 1994 enabled them to say they had nothing to do with the solicitation of hush money because they didn't know that Hubbell faced prosecution. But it is a lie, Kincaid says, that could come back to haunt them.

In sum, if you see a chopped down cherry tree, ask someone else if they did it if you want a straight answer.

Aspects of
Her Character—
Or Absence Thereof

* * * * * * * * * * * * * * * * *

"In today's *New York Post* a man
who went to Oxford with former President
Clinton claims that at the time both he and
Clinton dated a woman who turned out to be a
radical lesbian. After hearing this,
President Clinton said, 'Yeah, but only
one of us married her'."

—Conan O'Brien

Sometimes you can tell what a person is like by what she says, and sometimes by what she does, and sometimes a blend of both. Following is a series of verbal snapshots that, collectively, give indication of what she's really like. It adds up to a four letter word: yuck.

TASTELESSNESS

- In 1999, after the wife of terrorist Yassar Arafat told the co-president that Israel was deliberately poisoning Palestinians, Hillary embraced her.
- At a Martin Luther King, Jr., celebration Hillary said Republicans were running "the House" like a "plantation." Pulitzer Prize winning journalist Michael Goodwin called it "rancid race baiting."
- During her years in Arkansas, when Bill was king and she was a cuckold, the Clintons honored Dr. King while at the same time honoring Robert E. Lee, the Confederate general who fought to allow the South to keep blacks enslaved. What a combo!

TOUGHNESS

Before she threw her hairdo in the ring, a front-page story in *USA Today*—"Can Hillary Be Elected Commander in Chief?"—explored the issue and presented a poll that *Newsmax* boiled down:

- Only 36 percent said she could handle the situation in Iraq if elected president.

- Just 38 percent said she would effectively protect the country from terrorist attack.
- 59 percent thought Clinton is not strong on national security.
- 42 percent said she would use military force wisely as president.
- 56 percent doubted she could handle an international crisis.
- Only half said she is a strong and decisive leader.

Overall, 37 percent said they "strongly disagree" or "somewhat disagree" with the statement "Hillary Clinton is tough enough to President."

At the time, Washington insiders say Clinton repositioned herself to beef up her standing as a strong supporter of the military and a person who could be an effective commander in chief. She is the first New York senator to sit on the Armed Services Committee, and recently introduced legislation to boost the Army by 80,000 soldiers over the next four years.

She was nominated by the Pentagon—"with which her husband often had contentious relations, particularly on gays in the military"—to serve on a blue-ribbon panel studying how to foster better cooperation among the military services, *USA Today* reports.

Some GOP analysts say Hillary's decision not to divorce her husband after he admitted having an affair with Monica Lewinsky, which garnered sympathy from voters during her run for the Senate, could raise questions about her toughness. "She's going to have a problem in reconciling voters' pity for her plight as first lady with seeing her as a figure with heft on foreign policy and defense issues," said GOP pollster Kellyanne Conway.

LIBERALISM

A study by *National Journal* showed Clinton's record on defense, foreign policy and economics last year made her the 34th most liberal senator, while in 2003 she had ranked ninth. Obviously Clinton's recent shift smacked of a political makeover aimed at polishing her national security credentials before the 2008 run.

"I think these are absolutely newfound views," William Black, executive director of the anti-Clinton political action committee Stop Her Now, told *USA Today*. "This is someone coming from an administration that had open disdain for the military. Her whole involvement in getting on the Armed Services Committee is a calculated political ploy to burnish up her national security and defense credentials. She certainly didn't seem to care a whit about the military before."

★ ★ ★ ★ ★ ★ ★ ★ ★ ★ ★ ★ ★ ★ ★

How Clinton Rates

Through 2006, she has a lifetime 96 percent "Liberal Quotient" from Americans for Democratic Action.

ProgressivePunch gives her a 91.4 percent lifetime progressive rating, ranking her the 28th most progressive of current senators.

Through 2006, she has a lifetime 9 percent rating from the American Conservative Union.

She received an 'A' (excellent) on the Drum Major Institute's 2005 Congressional Scorecard on middle-class issues.

The American Civil Liberties Union has given her a 75 percent lifetime rating through September 2007.

Americans for Better Immigration has given her a lifetime grade of 'D-' through October 2007 on their Immigration-Reduction Report Card.

NARAL Pro-Choice America consistently gave her a 100 percent pro-choice rating from 2002 to 2006.

The National Rifle Association gave her an 'F' rating in 2006 for her stance on Second Amendment issues.

★ ★ ★ ★ ★ ★ ★ ★ ★ ★ ★ ★ ★ ★ ★ ★

CHEAPNESS

According to the *Drudge Report*, one day while campaigning for the U.S. Senate, Hillary "It Takes a Village" Clinton delivered a speech in which she lamented the sorry fact that New York's farmers were "really hurting these days." She and her motorcade then stopped for breakfast at the Village House, a favorite diner in Albion (an upstate farming town), where she enjoyed two orders of scrambled eggs, home fries, and rye toast. Her breakfast, said the restaurant, was on the house.

Clinton, who once declared a 15-cent income-tax deduction for a pair of her husband's underwear which had been donated to a charity, then left the waitress (a single mother on minimum wage) . . . no tip.

> "At a diner in upstate New York Hillary Clinton stiffed the waitress," Jay Leno remarked. "Usually It's Bill who does that . . ."
>
> —*The Drudge Report*, February, 2000

WACKINESS

In his book, *Unlimited Access*, former FBI agent Gary Aldrich, who was stationed at the White House when the Clintons were in power, tells of getting a call one day from a friend of his named Karen. They exchanged small talk, and then Karen asked about Hillary, whether or not she was "wacky." Aldrich asked her to explain and she said that a friend of hers who was a lobbyist was hired by three health insurance executives to arrange an interview—his sister knew Hillary from school—and to go with them when they presented what they considered their solution to the health care crisis. They had sent in advance copies of their plan, and had succeeded in getting an interview with Hillary.

Upon arrival at the White House they were ushered into and told to wait in the Roosevelt Room, where they waited for the First Lady to show up. Finally, an hour later, she did, their proposal in hand. She walked over to a table, slammed the document on it, and hissed:

"Gentlemen, I have looked at your proposal and it's pure bullshit. Now, you've had your meeting. Get out!"

Karen's lobbyist friend, pissed and mortified, got up from his chair and stared at Hillary.

"Mrs. Clinton," he said, "my sister warned me about you when she set up this meeting for me. She told me I would be sorry that I ever asked her to set this up, because she said you are a real bitch. She was wrong! You're a *fucking* bitch!" And with that, stormed out.

Later, while not confirming that Hillary was crazy, Aldrich would certainly agree with the lobbyist on her being a bitch.

BULLHEADEDNESS

Of course Hillary's greatest boondoggle thus far has been her healthcare plan. And while many people know that the plan was fatally flawed from the start, what many don't know is the aspect of her actions—or lack of actions—which grew out of her bullheadedness. This was revealed on the October 27, 2007, airing of CNBC's *The Russert Show*, during a discussion he had with Sally Bedell Smith, author of the book *For Love of Politics: Bill and Hillary Clinton: The White House Years*.

Russert: On health care, when you read the inside reporting in your book about it, it is so striking that there are significant people in the Clinton administration, the Secretary of the Treasury Lloyd Bentsen; the economic adviser Robert Rubin—I read somewhere that Donna Shalala, the Health and Human Services secretary, called the plan "crazy"; Leon Panetta, the Office of Management and Budget; [then-Senator] Pat Moynihan [D-NY], the chairman of the [Senate] Finance Committee; [then-Senator] Bill Bradley [NJ], another Democrat; Republicans, all saying, "We can do something, but this plan is too big, too much. Compromise, and we can get a scaled measure through." Ironically, the scaled-down plan they were talking about then is pretty close to the plan that Hillary has now adopted in 2008. Which means that from 1993 to 2008, 40 million people went without care because she was so wedded to getting that plan—her original plan—through. Fair?"

Bedell Smith: Absolutely fair. There were so many points along the way, and the complication again had to do with this dynamic between the two of them back then. There was a fellow who used to represent the hospitals named Michael Bromberg, and he said, "There was Hillary's White House and Bill's White House, and we didn't know which White House was in charge. And, as you say, if Hillary's White House had yielded to Bill's White House, we would've had a decent healthcare plan that would've worked for so many people. And I think the lesson, or the cautionary tale to look at, is the degree to which Hillary becomes invested in something she believes in, which was certainly the case then, and the test of that with this current plan, which, you know, has features that may be debatable, whether she would be willing to yield on things that Democrats—moderate Democrats, moderate Republicans would say to her 'these won't work.'" Would she be willing to fold them and accept something less? And that's the real crux of it, I think. It's not so much what she says, it's what she's willing to do. You have to look at the actions.

> **"Yesterday, Hillary Clinton criticized a neighbor in Chappaqua because the neighbor's son threw a party for his high school football team and had a stripper put on a nude sex show. President Clinton criticized the parents too, but only because he wasn't invited."**

—Conan O'Brien

"It's important to have core principles and values, but if you're going to be active in policy and politics, you have to be a realist."

—Hillary Clinton

"Here is the basic difference between the Bush family and the Clinton family. When Bill Clinton said it was time for a cold one, he meant Hillary."

—Jay Leno

"Former President Bill Clinton is in India right now and he is doing everything you do when you go to India. They put a turban on him and they had Bill Clinton riding an elephant. It's the biggest thing he's ridden since—well . . ."

—David Letterman

CRUDITY

- On Labor Day, 1991, while in the governor's mansion, Hillary asked her staff: "Where is that goddamn fucking flag? . . . I want the goddamn fucking flag up every fucking morning at fucking sunrise."—*Inside the White House,* p. 244.

- No love was lost between Hillary and the state troopers who guarded her in Arkansas. Once, after one said "good morning" to her, she responded: "Fuck off! It's enough that I have to see you shit-kickers every day. I'm not going to talk to you, too. Just do your goddamn job and keep your mouth shut."—*American Evita,* p. 90.

- One day Hillary told one of the Secret Service agents to carry her bags but he declined because he wanted to keep his hands free to go to his weapon, or prevent something bad from happening. Hillary didn't like it. "If you want to remain on this detail," she said, "get your fucking ass over here and grab those bags."—*The First Partner,* p. 259.

- Favorite Hillary obscenities that she used with the Secret Service included "Get the fuck out of my way!", "Get fucked," or "Get out of my face!"—*Hillary's Scheme*, p. 89.

- Another time Hillary felt she was being crowded by the Secret Service and yelled, "Stay the fuck back, stay the fuck away from me! Don't come within ten

yards of me . . . Just fucking do as I say, okay?"
—*Unlimited Access,* p. 139.

- Once a supporter of her husband gave her a pair of earrings shaped liked Arkansas Razorbacks. When the supporter was out of hearing she said: "This is the kind of shit I have to put up with."—*Blood Sport*

- Hillary didn't like the way Bill offered government jobs to troopers to keep silent about his womanizing, and she said, "Shit Bill, even Nixon wasn't that stupid."— *American Evita,* p. 136.

- On Inauguration Day, Hillary ripped into Bill Clinton twice, once saying "You fucking asshole," as reported in *Hillary's Choice* on page 223, and the other time she said, "You stupid motherfucker," which was reported in *The Seduction of Hillary Rodham.*

- In the middle of Hillary's healthcare debacle, President Clinton decided to try to get a healthcare plan that was different from hers. When she found out, she told him over the phone, "What the fuck are you doing up there? You get back here right away!" (And he did)—*The Survivor,* p. 18.

REVENGE

Public Relations specialist Robert Boostin, who worked with Hillary Clinton when she was trying to reform health care in America got to know both the Clintons well. Boostin told author Gail Sheehy, who wrote *Hillary's*

Choice. "He blows up and in the next five minutes loves you again. She gets angry at you and doesn't forget it for twenty years. Hillary is capable of carrying a grudge like almost no one I know. You're either with her or against her—black and white."

Indeed, Paula Jones, Juanita Broaddrick, Kathleen Willey, and Elizabeth Ward Gracen and others who were involved in a sexual way with Clinton were harassed by both Clintons by having their tax returns audited. It's all detailed by Candace E. Jackson in her book, *The Women Targeted by the Clinton Machine*: Hillary ". . . was right there in the inner circle taking a lead in giving these women zero credibility, in attacking them in public and through the press and in participating in all of these scare tactics, like hiring private investigators to threaten them and follow them . . . [she] is either as misogynistic as her husband or she is simply willing to conspire to mistreat women if that's what it takes to preserve their political careers."

LIKABILITY

Some critics have called her angry, impatient, given to temper outbursts, calculating, opportunistic, and a chronic victim, but Tim Cavanaugh of www.reason.com said, "Plainly put, it's her personality. She still lacks a key quality that a politician can't achieve through hard work: likability." Indeed, it's difficult to like someone who constantly patronizes her audiences, speaking ever so slowly so that the stupid masses will "get" what the smartest woman in the world is saying. Or when she uses her alienating alternative oratorical style, which consists solely of the strident, the screechy, and the preachy.

Other Nasty Scandals

* * * * * * * * * * * * * * * *

"How do you spell scandal? I don't know,
ask the Clintons. They know it by heart."

—Comedian Scott Booker

While the sex scandals that Billary was involved in leads the hit parade in terms of sheer infamy, there were other scandals that Hillary was involved in. Following are some of the more major ones:

THE MAGIC INVESTMENT This occurred after Bill Clinton became governor of Arkansas. Hillary invested the lordly sum of $1,000 with a commodities broker named Robert L. "Red" Bone, and she was able to turn a

$99,537 profit—in about a year. How? She said she did so by studying the *Wall Street Journal.* That response has about as much credibility as someone peddling snake oil, and the likelihood of someone being able to do that is zero. Indeed, a Chicago-based investment counselor told Barbara Olson in her book *Hell to Pay* that the average retail customer has ". . . as much chance of that kind of success as I have of driving to Hawaii."

Author Edward Klein says Hillary lied, that the almost 100,000 percent profit was facilitated by Arkansas power brokers who wanted to make sure they were in good standing with her newly-elected husband. In other words, it was a payoff, and that if they had not been behind her, she would have lost all her money. The brokers who helped get her such an obscene return on her investment were later prosecuted for using the same methods to turn a big profit.

WHITEWATER This became a symbol of greed and duplicity. Details on Whitewater were first publicized in 1992 in the *New York Times* in a series of articles written by Jeff Gerth, and in the midst of Bill Clinton's presidential campaign . . . and continued throughout Hillary's time as First Lady. Whitewater referred to a parcel of land near Flippin, Arkansas, that they had partnered up with Jim McDougal and his wife, Susan, to develop into housing.

It didn't work out for the Clintons; they had lost their late-investment in the Whitewater Development Corporation with the McDougals who also operated Madison Guaranty, a savings and loan institution that retained the legal services of Rose law firm—where Hillary was a partner—which may have been improperly subsidizing Whitewater losses. Madison Guaranty later failed, and Clinton's work at Rose was scrutinized for a possible conflict of interest in representing the bank before state regulators that her husband, the governor, had appointed. She claimed she had done minimal work for the bank. Independent counsels Robert Fiske and Kenneth Starr subpoenaed Clinton's legal billing records and she claimed to be unable to produce them. The records were later found in the First Lady's White House book room after a two-year search, and delivered to investigators in early 1996. The delayed appearance of the records sparked intense interest and another investigation about how they surfaced and where they had been; Clinton attributed the problem to disorganization that resulted from their move from the Arkansas governor's mansion and the effects of a White House renovation. After the discovery of the records, on January 26, 1996, Clinton made history by becoming the first First Lady to be subpoenaed to testify before a Federal grand jury. After several independent counsels investigated, a final report was issued in 2000 which stated that there was insufficient evidence that either Clinton had engaged in criminal wrongdoing. Some people felt there was some involvement, but no proof. Also, Hillary denied being even involved in Whitewater in any substantial way, though ultimately it came out that she had done sixty hours worth of work on it when she had been a member of Rose law firm. To this day, Whitewater retains its stench.

FILEGATE In 1993, a man named Craig Livingstone, a person with impeccable credentials, was an official in the White House office of personnel security. He collected several hundred background files on Republican opponents. The assumption by many people was that he had done this on orders from Hillary, but she said that she didn't know him. Maybe she didn't. But one day in a White House hallway Hillary was spotted by an intern hugging Livingstone. Maybe he had a twin.

TRAVELGATE Travelgate could also have been described as "The Bloodbath." It was like a scene out of the Godfather. To wit, one day in 1993, Hillary fired the entire staff—some of them with decades worth of experience—in the White House travel office. These were the people who handled lucrative travel arrangements for the press traveling with the Clintons.

The ostensible reason was that an internal audit on the office found it to be grossly mismanaged so Hillary, instead of giving the employees time to clean up their act, wielded the ax.

But as is so often the case with Hillary, many pundits said that she had an ulterior motive. According to White House insider David Watkins, Hillary dismissed the staff so she could give the jobs to the Clintons' Arkansas friends, Linda Bloodworth Thomason and Harry Thomason. Indeed, Watkins stated in a memo that there would be "hell to pay" if her travel office orders were not followed. And she said to him on the phone five days before the bloodbath as reported Barbara Olson's book *Hell to Pay* on page 242, "We need these people out—we need our people in—we need the slots."

ILLEGAL CONTRIBUTIONS Here, illegal contributions were made in the name of the smarmy game. Hillary denied knowing anything about the pedigree of the contributors, but if she wasn't lying then she was a fool. She should have. In 1996, while running for president, Bill Clinton received substantial contributions from two gentlemen named Johnnie Chung and Charlie Trie. Hillary maintains her staff did not vet Johnnie and Charlie, and the Clintons were left with great gobs of egg on their faces when they learned that Johnnie and Charlie were actually getting the money from the Chinese government—which tells a lot about how China felt about Bill Clinton's politics.

The other possible reason was desperation for money. Pick your poison. But Hillary vowed from that time on she would make sure that any political campaign the Clintons were involved in would only be supported by clean money.

Wrong. In her own presidential campaign in 2007, either she was desperate for money or the vetting was not done carefully enough. Another contributor, this one named Norman Hsu, who was of Chinese extraction and a large campaign contributor to Clinton's presidential campaign, was wanted in California for failing to appear for sentencing on a 1991 grand theft charge. On August 29, Clinton's campaign said that it would give the $23,000 that Hsu donated to charity.

★ ★ ★ ★ ★ ★ ★ ★ ★ ★ ★ ★ ★ ★ ★ ★

Criminal and Near Criminal Acts by the Clintons, Friends, and Associates

The Liberal Progressive Review compiled a list of the Clintons' criminal and near criminal acts and the friends and associates who had been involved in them.

- Most number of convictions and guilty pleas by friends and associates.
- Most number of cabinet officials to come under criminal investigation.
- Most number of witnesses to flee country or refuse to testify.
- Most number of witnesses to die suddenly.
- First President sued for sexual harassment.
- First President accused of rape.

- First President to be held in contempt of court.
- First President to be impeached for personal malfeasance.
- First First Lady to come under criminal investigation.
- Largest criminal plea agreement in an illegal campaign-contribution case.
- Greatest number of illegal campaign contributions.
- Number of Starr–Ray investigation convictions or guilty pleas to date: one governor, one associate attorney general and two Clinton business partners: 14.
- Number of Cabinet members who came under criminal investigation: 5.
- Number of individuals and businesses associated with the Clinton machine that were convicted of or pleaded guilty to crimes: 47.
- Number of these convictions during Clinton's presidency: 33.
- Number of indictments/misdemeanor charges: 61.
- Number of congressional witnesses who pleaded the Fifth Amendment, fled the country to avoid testifying, or (in the case of foreign witnesses) refused to be interviewed: 122.
- Guilty pleas and convictions obtained by Donald Smaltz in cases involving charges of bribery and fraud against former Agriculture Secretary Mike Espy and associated individuals and businesses: 15; acquitted or overturned cases (including Espy): 6.

- Clinton machine crimes for which convictions were obtained: drug trafficking, 3; racketeering, extortion, bribery, 4; tax evasion, kickbacks, embezzlement, 2; fraud, 12; conspiracy, 5; fraudulent loans, illegal gifts, 1; illegal campaign contributions, 5; money laundering, 6; perjury, et al.

- Number of times that Clinton figures who testified in court or before Congress said that they didn't remember, didn't know, or something similar: Bill Kennedy, 116; Harold Ickes, 148; Ricki Seidman, 160; Bruce Lindsey, 161; Bill Burton, 191; Mark Gearan, 221; Mack McLarty, 233; Neil Egglseston, 250; John Podesta, 264; Jennifer O'Connor, 343; Dwight Holton 348; Patsy Thomasson, 420; Jeff Eller, 697; and Hillary Clinton, 250.

★ ★ ★ ★ ★ ★ ★ ★ ★ ★ ★ ★ ★ ★ ★ ★

For Love of Money

Hillary loves campaign donations the way fish love water. Who can forget Hillary's "advice" to her husband in the middle of the 1996 fundraising season for that year's election? When President Clinton complained to Hillary that he was tired of attending all those fundraisers, she told him, "You're getting your a** out there and doing what has to be done. We need the money!" Years later, when candidate Hillary pulled up to a fundraiser in her "home" state of New York, she noticed the people in attendance were not  high rollers but locals and farmers. She snapped at an aide, "What the [expletive] did we come here for? There's no money here!"

And it's not just campaign donations—this former law firm partner and Wal-Mart board member loves money from all sources. When Jim and Susan McDougal offered to buy out the Clintons from the Whitewater land scheme, Hillary rejected their offer as too low: "No! Jim told me that this was going to pay for college for Chelsea. I still expect it to do that!" She also approached Dick Morris about allowing various "Friends of Bill" to pay for the construction of a swimming pool at the Arkansas governor's mansion, asking, "Why should my daughter not have a pool just because my husband is governor?" And while Hillary modestly down-played the $100,000 she claims to have earned playing the complicated cattle futures market by saying, "I was lucky." She proudly defended her $8 million book deal, proclaiming, "My agreement with Simon & Schuster fully complies with the Senate ethics rules."

—Thomas Kuiper

★ ★ ★ ★ ★ ★ ★ ★ ★ ★ ★ ★ ★ ★ ★

> Once a disheveled woman upstate asked Hillary if she had any food, prompting Hillary to reply with the only thing that came to mind. "My name is Hillary Clinton. You going to vote in the primary?"

—Famous joke about Hillary

FREE GIFTS

There is good reason for the legislation that bars senators and congressmen from receiving gifts valued at more than $50. Gifts are the currency of bribery in Washington. As Dick Morris said in *Rewriting History*: "give a politician a paper bag full of twenty dollar bills and you insult his integrity. Hand him an oriental vase worth as much, and he'll consider you a friend. Most elected officials are very careful about receiving gifts. The implication of favoritism and influence peddling may adhere long after the gift is consigned to the closet shelf."

But Hillary Clinton was not careful, and she received over $200,000 in gifts, most in the few weeks before her election, says Dick Morris, and taking office simply because she was legally allowed to do so. Following are a list of donations and the people who gave them to her, as reported in Morris's book:

- Barbara Allen, Belfast, Northern Ireland, $650 watercolor of Clinton ancestral homestead
- Georgetown Alumni, class of 1968, $38,000 Dale Chihuly basket set
- Arthur Athis, Los Angeles, California, $2,400 dining chairs
- Denudes Badarch, Ulan Bator, Mongolia, $1,300 drawings of Mongolian landscapes
- Robert Berks, Orient, New York, $2,500 bust of Harry Truman
- Bruce Bernson, Santa Barbara, California, $300 golf putter
- Mr. and Mrs. Bill Brandt, Winnetka, Illinois, $5,000 china
- Ken Burns, Walpole, New Hampshire, $800 photograph of Duke Ellington
- Ely Callaway, Carlsbad, California, $499 golf driver
- Iris Cantor, New York, New York, $4,992 china
- Robin Carnahan and Nina Ganci, St. Louis, Missouri, $340 two sweaters
- Glen Eden Carpets, Calhoun, Georgia, $6,282 two carpets
- Dale Chihuly, Seattle, Washington, $22,000 glass sculpture
- Ted Danson and Mary Steenburgen, $4,800 china
- Colette D'Etremont, New Brunswick, Canada, $300 flatware

- Dennis Doucette, Coral Gables, Florida, $310 golf bag, clothing, book
- Ronald and Beth Dozoretz, $7,000, dining room table, server, and golf clubs (Beth Dozoretz is a friend of Denise Rich, who spoke to the president about the Marc Rich pardon)
- Martin Patrick Evans, Chicago, Illinois, $5,000 rug
- Paul Goldenberg, La Habra, California, $2,993 TV and DVD player
- Myra Greenspun, Green Valley, Nevada, $1,588 flatware
- Vinod Gupta, Omaha, Nebraska, $450 leather jacket
- Richard C. Helmstetter, Carlsbad, California, $525 golf driver and balls
- Hal Hunnicutt, Conway, Arkansas, $360 golf irons
- Ghada Irani, Los Angeles, California, $4,944 flatware
- Jill and Ken Iscol, Pound Ridge, New York, $2,110 china and jacket
- Mr. and Mrs. Walter Kaye, New York, New York, $9,683 cigar travel humidor, china cabinet, and copy of President Lincoln's Cooper Union speech
- David Garriff, North Yorkshire, United Kingdom, $300 golf driver
- Steve Leutkehans, Morton Grove, Illinois, $650 golf driver

- David Martinous, Little Rock, Arkansas, $1,000 needlepoint rug
- Steve Mittman, New York, New York, $19,900 two sofas, easy chair, and ottoman
- Katsuhiro Miura, Japan, $500 golf driver
- Jan Munro, Sarasota, Florida, $650 painting of New York City
- Brad Noe, High Point, North Carolina, $2,843 sofa
- Margaret O'Leary, San Francisco, California, $595 pantsuit and sweater
- Mr. and Mrs. Joe Panko, Concord, North Carolina, $300 three putters
- Mr. and Mrs. Paolo Papini, Florence, Italy, $425 Italian leather box
- Mr. and Mrs. Morris Pynoos, Beverly Hills, California, $5,767 cashmere shawl and flatware
- Brian Ready, Chappaqua, New York, $300 painting of Buddy, the Clintons' dog
- Denise Rich, ex-wife of fugitive Marc Rich, $7,300 coffee table and chairs (Ms. Rich also donated $450,000 to the Clinton Presidential Library, $ 72,000 to the Hillary Clinton campaign and committees supporting her candidacy, $1 million to the Democratic Party and its candidates, and $10,000 to the Clintons' legal defense fund.)
- David Rowland, Springfield, Illinois, $500 check signed by President Harry Truman in 1934

- Stuart Shiller, Haileah, Florida, $1,170 lamps
- Steven Spielberg, $4,920 china
- Sylvester Stallone, $300 boxing gloves
- Mr. and Mrs. Vo Viet Thanh, Ho Chi Minh City, Vietnam, $350 framed tapestry
- Joan Tumpson, Miami, Florida, $3,000 painting
- Edith Wasserman, Beverly Hills, California, $4,967 flatware
- Mr. and Mrs. Allen Whiting, West Tisbury, Massachusetts, $300 painting
- James Lee Witt, Alexandria, Virginia, $450 cowboy boots
- Mr. and Mrs. Bud Yorkin, Los Angeles, California, $500 antique book on President Washington

CHAPTER 6

Carpetbagger

★ ★ ★ ★ ★ ★ ★ ★ ★ ★ ★ ★ ★ ★ ★ ★

"One big reason why people hate Hillary is that she was so calculating in running for the Senate in New York. It felt like a con job all the way."

—Thomas Williams

As Edward Klein reports in great detail in his book, *The Truth About Hillary*, Hillary got some good news in early November of 1998. Newsman Gabe Pressman of the local WNBC station sat down to interview the four-time Senator from New York, Daniel Patrick Moynihan, a man who had authored eighteen books, received sixty honorary degrees, and was famed for his high intellect.

At one point, the conversation turned to Moynihan's future.

"How do you feel about running again," Pressman asked, "or haven't you made up your mind?"

In posing the question, Pressman had to wonder if Moynihan knew that Democratic strategists were not too enthused with the prospect of Moynihan running again. He was a man who loathed fund-raisers, had little political money in the bank and hardly seemed geared up for a fifth campaign.

"Gabe," he said, "…I've served four terms in the Senate…let it stay at that. That's the longest term any New Yorker has ever served."

"As a lot of people hoped," Klein said, "Moynihan was going to retire."

Pressman was going to tell the world his exclusive on his Sunday morning show, but, not unpredictably, word leaked out almost immediately—and the political bandwagon started rolling as well.

Charles Rangel, the raspy-voiced powerhouse congressman who had served the people of Harlem for decades, called the White House and spoke to Hillary. He told her the news and said that he hoped she would run as a candidate from New York State.

Hillary did not sound so enthusiastic about the prospect. Still reeling from Monicagate, she created the impression that she was more concerned with the state of her marriage and with the condition that the presidency was in.

But that was the surface Hillary. Inside, she was, of course, calculating—and in fact had been calculating since the previous fall by barnstorming the country helping fellow Democrats. She was well aware that there might be an empty Senate seat in 2000 and she wanted to be able to park her ample derriere in it.

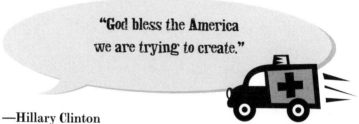

"God bless the America we are trying to create."

—Hillary Clinton

A minor detail, of course, was that her home state was Illinois, but she wouldn't want to try to run there because she wasn't very popular. In New York State the last popularity poll had her at a healthy 56 percent.

The best move, she calculated, in her run was to align forces with New York candidate Chuck Schumer, who would be running against Senator Al D'Amato, a power-house senator.

Klein said Charles Rangel felt, as he told Hillary, that no one could beat her and he used a friend of his, Bob Herbert— the only African American on the op-ed page of the *New York Times* to write, just six days after Moynihan's announcement, beseeching Hillary to run.

Hillary of course didn't need any beseeching. She was ready to run. But as Klein points out, politics in New York is akin to maximum fighting, that it is no holds barred, and the candidates were expected to let it all hang out. This could be a big problem for Hillary because secrecy and deception were as natural to her as breathing, and the New York media would dig like mad dogs to get the answers.

In order to win the nomination, Hillary had two big jobs: convince the county leaders that she could do a good job as senator, and convince New Yorkers that she understood their problems and was not someone who would sweep in from the outside supposedly armed with solutions to problems she knew nothing about.

Hillary did a good job to start, Klein says, hiring a woman named Judith Hope to talk to county leaders—i.e., the leaders of the counties with the most votes—and ask them not to prejudge Hillary, to give her a chance before they started making negative statements. Hope did a good job, and broke ground as well as it could be broken.

Though New York State is huge—nineteen million people living in 54,000 square miles of land—Hillary vowed to visit as many places as she could, typically speaking in a hall with a crowd in front of her talking to them about their problems. It was called a "listening tour" and it was a clever way to find out what the problems in the state were, and to show the citizens that she was not as "cold, mean and tough" as people had read about her, that she did not have horns—at least not growing out of her head.

But the biggest problem was getting the support of what Edward Klein characterized as the "Big Kahuna," Pat Moynihan.

The problem was that neither Moynihan nor his wife, Liz, who managed his successful campaigns, liked her, nor she them. Still, as politics goes, one day she traveled to Moynihan's condo in Washington to meet with Pat and Liz and ultimately, get their blessings. As it happened, the meeting was a disaster.

People often charge that Hillary is a know-nothing carpetbagger, and are always looking for evidence to support this. On an appearance on the *David Letterman Show,* Letterman grilled Hillary, as reported by Peggy Noonan in her book *The Case Against Hillary Clinton*: "[Letterman] asks her the name of the [New York] state bird. "The bluebird" she says to applause. The state tree? Hillary gets a *Jeopardy* Daily Double look. "Um, the maple." "But which maple?" She blinks, thinking hard. "Let's see, there's red maple, the sugar maple . . ." "That's it!" says Letterman to more applause. The next day, it turns out she had seen the questions in advance and thus not only were her answers but her Daily Double look a calculated fraud on the audience."

While campaigning for a seat in the New York senate, Hillary Clinton, an Illinois native, faced accusations of carpetbagging. *The San Francisco Chronicle's* Leah Garchik, for example, reported that a tractor company in New York was selling a Hillary Clinton manure spreader. "And like its namesake," she dryly observed, "it's not made in New York."

It was likely doomed from the start. The break between Hillary and the Moynihan's had really started way back in 1992. Moynihan had urged Clinton to push through Welfare reform, which had many supporters in Congress, and once this was done it would be easier to push through a healthcare package.

But Clinton instead started with the complex and difficult bill on health care, and Moynihan was convinced that he did so because he was persuaded by Hillary. He also bungled by putting Hillary, who had no experience at getting a bill like this through, in charge, and Hillary totally botched, by dint of her aggressive personality to push the bill through without first coddling and working with senators whose support was vital.

Moynihan thought he knew why: Hillary had taken on getting the bill through—not to help Americans get the health care they needed, but as means to shine a positive light on herself to increase her chances of succeeding Bill in the White House.

Moynihan also had found both Clintons difficult to deal with, and was insulted by their staff's failure to contact him on anything. When Hillary arrived that day to get his endorsement, both Moynihan and his wife were loaded for bear. As Klein said "He told friends that he had a long list of people he disliked in the Clinton administration and that at the top of the list was Hillary."

A number of times he had caught her lying. Indeed, she once told reporters that Pat Moynihan had never held hearings on her healthcare plan. Moynihan had held thirty meetings.

Liz Moynihan also disliked Hillary. She said of her "I believe that she believes God approves of her, and that therefore she can't do anything wrong."

The visit started badly with Hillary referring to the Moynihan's having seen the Dalai Lama and telling them how swept away she was by his "spirituality." Neither Liz nor Pat believed her. Liz had worked with Hillary and she wondered whether Clinton would run for Moynihan's Senate seat and both she and her husband, Klein said, "considered Hillary a liar and dissembler."

Eventually, the talk got to Pat's endorsement and Liz told Hillary that the reason Pat was successful was because he was a good candidate, "that people like him," as reported in Klein's book. Liz said that people didn't like Hillary because of her support of a Palestinian state and because of her healthcare plan, since there were many teaching hospitals in New York. Hillary then tried to claim that she had sponsored a bill that would protect the hospitals, but both Liz and Pat knew she was lying . . . because the bill she was referring to was Pat's.

In any event, Hillary left the house without Moynihan's support, a gap in her plan that could be fatal to her campaign.

But politics is politics, and Hillary fortunately had someone named Mandy Grunwald, a liberal whose father, Henry Grunwald, had been editor in chief of *Time* magazine, working for her. Mandy had a long-time good relationship with the Moynihans, and, after some superb convincing, got them to endorse Hillary in a grand pronouncement at their farm in Delaware County.

★ ★ ★ ★ ★ ★ ★ ★ ★ ★ ★ ★ ★ ★ ★

Embarrassing Moment

In February 2000, First Lady Hillary Clinton announced her candidacy for the U.S. Senate at the State University of New York at Purchase.

"I've heard parents' concerns about the media's influence on their children," Hillary declared during her announcement speech. "How to protect our children from the influence of popular culture . . ."

Ironically, moments before she took the stage, a curious warm-up song, specially selected by the Hillary Campaign, had blasted over the gathered crowd—and on to viewers nationwide via C-SPAN and CNN:

"Your sister's gone out, she's on a date, and you just sit at home and masturbate . . . So you go to the village in your tie-dye jeans. And you stare at the junkies and the closet queens. It's like some pornographic magazine, and you smile . . . So you play your albums and you smoke your pot. And you meet your girlfriend in the parking lot . . . Captain Jack will get you high tonight!"

"The campaign offers its sincerest apology for the mistake," a spokesman later said. "The First Lady does not endorse the message in the Billy Joel song."

—Source: *The Drudge Report,* February, 2000

★ ★ ★ ★ ★ ★ ★ ★ ★ ★ ★ ★ ★ ★ ★

If She Gets Elected, Be Afraid, Be Very Afraid…

★ ★ ★ ★ ★ ★ ★ ★ ★ ★ ★ ★ ★ ★ ★ ★ ★

There's a joke going around about Hillary Clinton that, at root, is chilling. It goes:

    Q: What's the difference between Hillary Clinton and Caesar Chavez of Venezuela?

    A: Hillary doesn't speak Spanish.

Hidden in the joke is more than a kernel of fear. People who fear Hillary fear her deeply. Many are well aware that her biggest boondoggle, Hillarycare, would have given everyone free or low-cost health care—and bankrupted the country.

But there are also very specific policies she is going to try to foist on the American public that will be hell to pay for in more ways than one.

Two new scenarios from the mind of Hillary particularly disturb Dick Morris, who once worked for the Clintons.

One is quite simple: she'll take some action that will bring on a depression, and even before she becomes president. As Morris explains it: "Hillary Clinton will cause the stock market to crash as her likely election as president approaches. She says she wants to raise the capital gains tax. Now it's 15 percent. She might hike it to 30 percent or she might eliminate it altogether and tax profits from sales of stock or houses as ordinary income at 40 percent. So what will happen? As election day approaches, smart investors will sell their stocks because they will want to pay 15 percent not 30 or 40 percent. They'll realize that if they wait, they'll just have to cough up more in taxes. That will cause stock prices to tank and with them our retirement savings. And that is only the start of the many gifts we'd get if Hillary becomes president. Only the start."

> **"Senator Obama's comment today is fundamentally at odds with what his teachers, family, classmates and staff have said about his plans to run for president. Senator Obama's campaign rhetoric is getting in the way of his reality."**

—Clinton campaign spokesman Phil Singer

PRESS RELEASE

Today in Iowa, Senator Barack Obama said: "I have not been planning to run for president for however many number of years some of the other candidates have been planning for."

However, the facts don't back up Sen. Obama's claim.

Immediately after joining the Senate, Sen. Obama started planning to run for President:

"'The first order of business for Obama's team was charting a course for his first two years in the Senate. The game plan was to send Obama into the 2007–2008 election cycle in the strongest form possible,' writes [David] Mendell in his forthcoming bio, *Obama: From Promise to Power.* **The final act of the plan was turning up the talk about a**

potential presidential bid, which was greatly aided by his positive press and suggestions by pundits that he run for president." [*U.S. News and World Report*, 6/19/07]

His law school classmates say that Sen. Obama has been planning presidential run for "more than a decade":

"[A]ccording to those who know him, **he has been talking about the presidency for more than a decade**. 'It was clear to me from the day I met him that he was thinking about politics,' says Harvard Law School classmate Christine Spurell." [*Washington Post*, 8/12/07]

Fifteen years ago, Sen. Obama told his brother-in-law he was planning to run for president:

Sen. Obama's brother-in-law, Craig [Robinson], pulled Sen. Obama aside [in 1992] and asked about his plans. "He said, 'I think I'd like to teach at some point in time, and maybe run for public office,' recalls Robinson, who assumed Obama meant he'd like to run for city alderman. 'He said no—at some point he'd like to run for the U.S. Senate. And then he said, '**Possibly even run for president** at some point.' And I was like, 'Okay, but don't say that to my Aunt Gracie.' I was protecting him from saying something that might embarrass him." [*Washington Post*, 8/12/07]

In third grade, Sen. Obama wrote an essay titled 'I Want To Be a President':

Sen. Obama's third grade teacher, Fermina Katarina Sinaga, "asked her class to write an essay titled 'My dream: What I want to be in the future.' Obama wrote

'**I want to be a president**,' she said." [*The Los Angeles Times*, 3/15/07]

In kindergarten, Sen. Obama wrote an essay titled 'I Want to Become President':

"Iis Darmawan, 63, Obama's kindergarten teacher, remembers him as an exceptionally tall and curly haired child who quickly picked up the local language and had sharp math skills. He wrote an essay titled, **'I Want To Become President**,' the teacher said." [*AP*, 1/25/07]

★ ★ ★ ★ ★ ★ ★ ★ ★ ★ ★ ★ ★ ★ ★

Morris also sees big problems with Hillary's new health-care plan because when Democrats and liberals speak of the 50 million uninsured Americans , more than one fifth of these are illegal immigrants!

"Hillary," Morris says, "also speaks of the importance of stopping health insurance companies from raising premiums on those who are sick. But she does not mention the inevitable flip side of her proposal—to raise premiums on those who are well."

Her program would also be compulsory. Even if you didn't want the insurance—you might be covered elsewhere—you would have to take it as a precondition of employment.

Another problem: Morris says "the main defect is that it leaves out any attempt at cost control with healthcare absorbing 16 percent of our economy." If there is no control, greed and deception will run rampant.

Morris sees a variety of reasons why Hillary can win the nomination and the election. In his book *Rewriting History*, a take off on her book *Living History*, he lists:

- The public relations triumph of her book and promotion tour
- A safe perch in the Senate, where the wounds of Whitewater and the other Clinton scandals are healing—and the memories are fading
- The dearth of potential Democratic rivals

★ ★ ★ ★ ★ ★ ★ ★ ★ ★ ★ ★ ★ ★ ★ ★

Who Hates Her More?

Polling evidence suggests that men remain significantly more hostile to Mrs. Clinton than women. About 45 percent of men have a negative opinion of her and only 36 percent have a positive opinion. The figures for women are almost the mirror opposite—31 percent negative to 45 percent positive.

★ ★ ★ ★ ★ ★ ★ ★ ★ ★ ★ ★ ★ ★ ★ ★

STOP HER NOW

Many groups are trying to stop Hillary as she scoots down the yellow brick road to the White House. Prominent among them is an organization called, appropriately enough, STOP HER NOW. This is a coalition of conservatives who are trying to knock her off that yellow brick road, dedicated to derailing her chances of capturing the Democratic nomination. "We're out to expose her as a confirmed left-wing radical, and life-long liberal who long ago sold her soul to the divisive, radical, and ultra-liberal special interest groups who see everyone as 'victims' and want to use your tax dollars and the power of the state to make things right," the group says on its website, STOP HER NOW.com.

Of course STOP HER NOW is not the only group that's trying. The following is a list of other sites:

1. Don't Elect Hillary
2. No Hillary 2008
3. The Hillary Project
4. Anyone But Hillary 2008!
5. Stop Hillary Pac
6. Hillary Watch
7. I Hillary
8. Exile From Hillary's Village
9. Gotta Stop Hillary

10. Conservative Rebel
11. Just My Opinion…But I'm Right
12. Conservative Nation
13. Anti-Liberal
14. Liberals Suck

"I have to confess that it's crossed my mind that you could not be a Republican and a Christian."

—Hillary Clinton

"I believe in evil, and I think that there are evil people in the world."

—Hillary Clinton, in 1993, stating her opinion not of the terrorists who had just bombed the World Trade Center, but of those who opposed her health care reform plan

★ ★ ★ ★ ★ ★ ★ ★ ★ ★ ★ ★ ★ ★ ★

Memo to Obama: Win Iowa or Lose the Race

TO: Senator Barack Obama

FROM: Karl Rove

SUBJECT: How to Beat Hillary

Not that you have asked for advice, but here it is anyway: Iowa is your chance to best her. If you do not do it there, odds are you never will anywhere. You are way behind her in most national polls. The only way to change that is to beat her in Iowa so people around America take another look at you. You did a smart thing organizing effectively in the early primary states. But you can take advantage of that only if you win Iowa and keep her from building an overwhelming sense of invincibility and inevitability.

The good news is you have again got "the buzz." Polls are looking better for you in Iowa and the other early states. Your press is improving, with your performance at the Iowa Jefferson-Jackson dinner a big help. Hillary Clinton has made unforced errors. But she is still the frontrunner and there are several things you need to do quickly to win.

First, stop acting like a vitamin-deficient Adlai Stevenson. Striking a pose of being high-minded and too pure will not work. Americans want to see you scrapping and fighting for the job, not in a mean or ugly way but in a forceful and straightforward way.

Hillary may come over as calculating and shifty but she looks in control. You, on the other hand, often come over as weak and

 ineffectual. In some debates, you do not even look at her when disagreeing with her, making it look as if you are afraid of her. She offers you openings time and again but you do not take advantage of them. Sharpen your attacks and make them more precise.

Take the exchange in the Philadelphia debate about Bill and Hillary keeping documents hidden about her role as first lady in his White House. She was evasive. You spoke next. You would have won a big victory if you had turned to her and said: "Senator, with all due respect, you and your husband could release those documents right now if you wanted to. Your failure to do so raises questions among a lot of Americans about what you're hiding and those questions would hurt our party if you were our nominee." But your response was as weak as dirty dishwater. Do not let other great opportunities pass by.

Second, focus on the fact that many Democrats have real doubts about Hillary. They worry she cannot win, will be a drag on the ticket, and that if she got to the White House it would be a disaster. You know better than most what they are worried about; they have told you their fears. It is why you have done so well raising money from Bill's backers and gaining support from Clinton administration officials. Talk about those doubts. Put them in a bigger context than just the two of you. Remind primary voters that these short-comings will hurt Democratic chances.

Third, when you create controversies do not pick issues where you are playing the weaker hand. For example, you attacked her for lacking foreign policy experience. It is true she was first lady, not secretary of state, and nobody will ever mistake her for James Baker III. But your qualifications are even thinner; you were a state senator and lived in Indonesia when you were six. Big deal. Americans think she has more foreign policy experience than you—and she does.

Fourth, when you disagree with her, be clear about what you believe. You cannot afford more garbled responses like the one you gave in Las Vegas on drivers' licenses for illegal aliens. Answer yes or no. Do not give voters evidence you are as calculating as her.

Fifth, you need to do a better job explaining what kind of change you represent. The change theme is a good one and Democratic voters know you were against the war and represent the idea of something fresh. But they do not know who you really are, what you want to do and where you want to take the country. Taking her down a few notches is step one; telling people who you are is the next. Both are necessary.

Sixth, find a way to gently belittle her whenever she tries to use disagreements among Democrats as an excuse to complain about being picked on. The toughest candidate in the field should not be able to complain when others disagree with her.

This is not a coronation. Democrats do not like her sense of entitlement. She is not owed the nomination. It does not belong to her simply because her name is Clinton. So blow the whistle on her when she tries to become a victim. Do it with humour and a smile and it will sting even more.

Hillary comes across as cold, distant, and conspiracy-minded, more like Richard Nixon than her sunny, charming husband. During the Clinton presidency she oversaw the Hillarycare disaster and argued hard against welfare reform, one of the promises on which he had campaigned. She is a hard-nosed competitor with a tough and seasoned staff.

But her record is weak, her personality off-putting, and her support thin. If she wins the nomination it will be because her rivals—namely you—were weak when you confronted her and could not look her in the eye when you did. She is beatable but you have to raise your game. Iowa is your great chance for a breakthrough. Win it convincingly and you can build on it in the contests that follow. Lose it and victory becomes much more difficult.

—Source: AOL. Karl Rove is a former senior adviser and deputy chief of staff to President George W. Bush and advised on his 2000 and 2004 presidential election campaigns

★ ★ ★ ★ ★ ★ ★ ★ ★ ★ ★ ★ ★ ★ ★ ★

PART 2
This 'n That

CHAPTER 8

The Nutcracker and Other Anti-Hillary Merchandise

★ ★ ★ ★ ★ ★ ★ ★ ★ ★ ★ ★ ★ ★ ★ ★ ★ ★

The outpouring of hate against Hillary is truly phenomenal, and one way it has been expressed is a variety of anti-Hillary merchandise. One of my favorites is a little item called "The Nutcracker," which is basically a 9-inch high real nutcracker that looks like Hillary. And it works. All you need to do is place the nut between her bowed, ridged metal thighs and squeeze. The nut cracks. It costs $2.95.

Another interesting item is the Hillary Voodoo Doll. The advertising copy says: "Yes, everybody seems to feel strongly about Hillary Clinton. But is anybody actually doing anything about her? Now you can wield influence over

Hillary Clinton in a way her party or Bill never have with the "Hillary Clinton Voodoo Kit! " Another item I particularly like is Hillary toilet paper, with her smiling image imprinted on the sheets. Another item: Hillary money, which looks like real U.S. currency but has Hillary's picture where you'd expect to see a president.

There are also T-shirts and bumper stickers and buttons galore available, which include cartoons or photos of Hillary along with biting sentiments.

A sampling:

- HILLARY 2008: EVEN BILL DOESN'T WANT HER
- HILLARY 2008: I WOULD CHEAT ON HER TOO
- HILLARY 2008: LIFE IS A BITCH, SO DON'T VOTE FOR ONE
- HILLARY 2008: IF SHE'S THE ANSWER . . . IT MUST HAVE BEEN A STUPID QUESTION
- HILLARY 2008: SHE SCARES ME
- HILLARY 2008: JUST SAY NYET

One that struck the author as particularly effective was a button with Hillary's picture on it and the sentence: SOME-WHERE IN ARKANSAS A VILLAGE IS MISSING THEIR IDIOT.

Following are some of the interesting items available in the market:

Hillary Nutcracker. (Courtesy of Prank Place.com)

Voodoo doll allows you to put the hex on Hillary. It comes with pins and instructions. (Courtesy of PrankPlace.com)

One of many anti-Hillary buttons.

Toilet paper (Courtesy of PrankPlace.com).

CHAPTER 9

Strictly for Laughs: Great Hillary Jokes

★ ★ ★ ★ ★ ★ ★ ★ ★ ★ ★ ★ ★ ★ ★

Late night talk shows and others lived on Bill Clinton's sexual indiscretions, his relationship with Hillary, and hers with him. Following is a sampling of jokes and some real-life funny stories:

✳ ✳ ✳ ✳ ✳ ✳

"President Clinton had quadruple bypass surgery over the weekend and is recovering nicely. The doctors told him he can resume having sex in about two weeks. And Hillary said, 'If he does, I'll kill him.'"—David Letterman

✳ ✳ ✳ ✳ ✳ ✳

"Hillary said during the Lewinsky scandal a lot of people reached out to her including the Dali Lama. The Dali Lama called her at the White House. He told her Bill's yin and yang were out of balance. The Dali Lama told her Bill was spending too much time on his yang."—Jay Leno

* * * * * *

"Hillary Clinton's new 506-page memoirs comes out next week. So much of her personality shines through that, in the end, you'll want to sleep with an intern."—Craig Kilborn

* * * * * *

One day Hillary and her chauffeur were driving along a back road when an old cow suddenly appeared in the road, and before he could stop the limo he slammed into the ancient bovine and killed it.

Hillary said:

"Find the person who owns the cow and tell them what happened."

Hillary stayed in the car while the driver went off to find the farmer.

Curiously, the driver was gone about an hour before returning, and he looked half drunk, was carrying an expensive bottle of champagne and was puffing on a big Cuban cigar, his clothes and hair in disarray. And he had a big smile on his lipstick-smeared face.

"What happened?" Hillary said.

"It was great," the driver said "I found the farmer and as soon as I told him what happened he pulled me inside the house, wined me and dined me and then led me to his two beautiful daughters who made passionate love to me."

"My God, what'd you say?"

"I said 'I'm Hillary Clinton's driver and I just killed the old cow.' The farmer pulled me inside the door and the rest happened so fast I couldn't stop it."

✳ ✳ ✳ ✳ ✳ ✳

"Yesterday, Hillary Clinton criticized a neighbor in Chappaqua because the neighbor's son threw a party for his high school football team and had a stripper put on a nude sex show. President Clinton criticized the parents too, but only because he wasn't invited."—Conan O'Brien

✳ ✳ ✳ ✳ ✳ ✳

"*Vanity Fair* magazine reports that former President Clinton and Al Gore haven't spoken to each other since George W. Bush's inauguration. Not only that, Bill and his wife, Hillary, haven't spoken since Richard Nixon's inauguration." —Conan O'Brien

✳ ✳ ✳ ✳ ✳ ✳

"Here is the basic difference between the Bush family and the Clinton family. When Bill Clinton said it was time for a cold one, he meant Hillary." —Jay Leno

* * * * * *

"According to ABC News, Bill Clinton often sneaks back to Washington to be with Hillary. I guess he doesn't want his girlfriends finding out that he is seeing his wife."
—Jay Leno

* * * * * *

"Yesterday at a White House ceremony, the official portrait of President Clinton was unveiled. Apparently, Clinton's portrait is so realistic that Hillary immediately started yelling at it."—Conan O'Brien

* * * * * *

"Bill Clinton's memoir, which is coming out in June, is called *My Life*. I believe it's an oral history. . . . They say it should be a good read even for people who are unfamiliar with Bill Clinton—you know, like Hillary."—Jay Leno

* * * * * *

"There's a cold front moving across the country. Yeah, it's Hillary starting her book tour"—Craig Kilborn

* * * * * *

"You may think you have a stressful job, but since she's been a senator, Hillary Clinton, they say, put on 30 pounds. In fact, she has gotten so heavy that today Bill hit on her."
—David Letterman

CHAPTER 10

How Do I Hate Thee?
Let Me Count
the Ways ...

★ ★ ★ ★ ★ ★ ★ ★ ★ ★ ★ ★ ★ ★ ★ ★ ★

Many years ago on *Family Feud*, one of the questions was "Who was the most hated person in history?" The most hated person—hated worse that Adolph Hitler—was Richard Nixon, then president. Today, if *Family Feud* asks that question, you can guess who will win.

Following are the thoughts and feelings of how some bloggers feel about her:

Five Good Ways to Make People Hurl Chunks

1. Watch Hillary walk wearing a thong bathing suit.
2. Listen to her talk about her new healthcare plan.

3. Watch her take the oath of office on Inauguration Day.
4. Watch her being sincere with soldiers.
5. Listen to her compliment her sexually addicted husband.

—Kenneth McGrath

Q: In mid November of 2007, Hillary announced that her campaign color was yellow. Did she think we'd be surprised?
A: Not at all.

Five Good Uses for Hillary's Butt

1. Visual aid to show how two worlds would look pressed together.
2. Visual aid to show the kind of female derriere Bill Clinton doesn't like.
3. Visual aid to show what a badly swollen avocado looks like.
4. Visual aid to show what two good watermelons look like.
5. Visual aid to show how effective a pantsuit is in hiding a derriere that's as big as a medicine ball.

–JoJo Cetrano

✢ ✢ ✢ ✢ ✢ ✢

BLOG GONE MILD: WHY DO THEY HATE HILLARY CLINTON SO MUCH?

The Truth said . . .

Hillary personifies all that is politics. She lies, she misrepresents, she slings mud, and she is very, very good at it. I hate her not because of her policies, everyone is entitled to their opinion. I hate her not because she knows how to play the game, I respect anyone who can accomplish their goals.

I hate her because she is so plastic, false, and mostly because dumb-nuts liberals buy into her ridiculous, superficial, insincere rhetoric. She knew about Bill's indiscretions, yet came on TV, cried and claimed she didn't know. She stole property from the Whitehouse (remember that Donkies?). She instituted a policy wherein people in the Whitehouse were not even allowed to look her in the face. Who does she think she is?

She thinks she's better than you! How completely arrogant. I think you Donkies need to get your heads out of your asses and wake up!

✢ ✢ ✢ ✢ ✢ ✢

Anonymous said . . .

Why the right doesn't like Hillary:

1. She seems willing to do virtually anything to get ahead. For ex. sticking with Bill because it enhanced

her chances for higher office even though she appeared to have little affection for him. Moving to NY to become a Senator. Losing/hiding/finding Rose law firm files. The list could be far longer, but you've heard it before.

2. She does not appear to have a world view grounded in a particular philosophy or moral system other than expediency.
3. She is bright and capable which is particularly dangerous when combined with 1 and 2 above.

She isn't loathed because she is a woman or a Clinton. She is loathed because she is perceived as amoral, Machiavellian, and dangerous for America.

✳ ✳ ✳ ✳ ✳ ✳

Cranny said . . .

Frankly, I think Hillary for prez in 2008 is the Republican party's best and only hope for the White House in the next election. As a life-long moderate Republican, I'm so disgusted with Bush the 2nd, that I'm voting democrat in 2008 . . . unless it Hillary on the ticket. I don't want to see a Republican in the White House in 2008, but "better the devil you know than the devil you don't." Hillary is so baldly political and insincere, that few really know what she really stands for . . .

✳ ✳ ✳ ✳ ✳ ✳

Demosthenes said . . .

The simple fact is, she voted FOR the war in Iraq. She now claims that if she were president at the time then she would NOT have done it. This means one of two things: Either she is a spineless coward who is too afraid to do anything and will only follow larger and people with stronger convictions around, or she will say whatever she think will win her the most votes.

⁂ ⁂ ⁂ ⁂ ⁂ ⁂

Aging But Still Lucid said . . .

"In the four years since the inspectors left, intelligence reports show that Saddam Hussein has worked to rebuild his chemical and biological weapons stock, his missile delivery capability, and his nuclear program. He has also given aid, comfort, and sanctuary to terrorists, including Al Qaeda members.. It is clear, however, that if left unchecked, Saddam Hussein will continue to increase his capacity to wage biological and chemical warfare, and will keep trying to develop nuclear weapons." —Sen. Hillary Clinton (D, NY), Oct. 10, 2002

⁂ ⁂ ⁂ ⁂ ⁂ ⁂

RetroCon said . . .

Bill had skill. They called him Slick Willie because he could pander, but when you examined his words, he hadn't really said anything.

Hillary's lack of nuance has made it clear, she's bought and paid for, by the far left, and the far left is not the democratic base.

She can't win the general election if she keeps pandering to the far left. But in the 'eat your own' world of secular progressives, she can't win the primary if she appears to be getting close to the aisle.

Rick said . . .

I hate Hillary because she probably profited from illegally "parked" commodities trades and then lied about it, because she probably engaged in illegally pushing her Waterwater debts onto her friend's bank, because subpoened documents turned up under her bed, because she is married to a creep (which by the transitive property makes her a creep too), because she's always saying stupid things like vast right wing conspiracy, because she is the most shrill person I've ever heard and because she has cankles.

A Gruesome Glossary

★ ★ ★ ★ ★ ★ ★ ★ ★ ★ ★ ★ ★ ★ ★ ★ ★

Addict, Sex. Is Bill Clinton a sex addict? It's a complicated subject, and some doctors don't even think the condition exists, though many do. One who does is Dr. Jennifer Schneider, who identified three indicators of sexual addiction: "compulsivity, continuation(of sexual activity) despite consequences, and obsession." Let's look at each one. *Compulsivity:* This is the loss of the ability to choose freely whether to stop or continue a behavior. *Continuation despite consequences:* When addicts take their addiction too far they may start withdrawing from family life to pursue sex. They put money, marriage, family, and career at risk for sex. *Obsession:* When the addict can't stop thinking particular thoughts. They constantly fantasize about sex, find new ways of obtaining it, and mentally revisit past experiences. Because of their obsession, their minds are held sexual captives and other areas of their lives are neglected. While we can't know for sure, if you look at Clinton's behavior in light of the conditions above, the question of whether he is a sex addict or not sure is interesting.

Alinsky, Saul. A radical leftward thinker, champion of the lower classes of society, whose philosophy and methods were fed to and adopted by Hillary Clinton. At the core of his philosophy was accumulating power, which one gathered any way one could, either by guile or using one's own power.

Billary. A name coined by journalists to describe what everyone knows: When Clinton was president he didn't run the government alone. The same will be true if Hillary gets to be president, of course.

Broaddrick, Juanita. In a gripping account punctuated by sobs on *Dateline* in 1999, Arkansas woman Juanita Broaddrick said that in her hotel room, (he) "turned me around and started kissing me, and that was a real shock. I first pushed him away. I just told him 'no.' . . . He tries to kiss me again. He starts biting on my lip. . . . And then he forced me down on the bed. I just was very frightened. I tried to get away from him. I told him 'no.' . . . He wouldn't listen to me."

She told this to *Dateline* 1999, 21 years after it happened in the Camelot Hotel in Little Rock, Arkansas. Her charge was never proved, but neither was it disproved. The man was Bill Clinton, at the time attorney general, the chief law enforcement officer of the state of Arkansas.

Carpetbagger. An odious description that Hillary was accused of being when she ran for the Senate in 2000. Her home state was Illinois—so she was convinced by Representative Charles Rangel and other politicos to run as a New York Senator. She therefore took up residence in New York State, and lived in New York for the required six months so she could run. Originally, she was to face Rudolph Giuliani, but he contracted prostate cancer and his personal life was in a shambles so he withdrew from the race. Hillary therefore ran against Long Islander Rick Lazio, a last minute substitute, and trounced him in the general election. One of the ways she did this was to travel upstate extensively where there was a heavy Republican base and convince them to vote for her.

Cigar. Famous as a sex object in Bill Clinton's affair with Monica Lewinsky. Clinton used cigars in place of a penis. Whether he also smoked them is not known.

Clinton, Bill. Twice elected president of the United States, 1992 and 1996. Born and raised in small-town Arkansas, he married Hillary Rodham and as president was almost impeached on obstruction of justice charges.

Clinton, Chelsea. The one and only child of the Clintons. On the surface, she seems to be a together young woman, but one wonders if what she went through watching her parents' marital difficulties has left her discouraged.

Fellatio. Who could have dreamed how important this act was to become in the life of the 42nd President of the United States? But it did, and it allowed Bill Clinton to legally deny having sex with Monica Lewinsky because Paula Jones's attorneys had described the sex act as intercourse. It is a ludicrous idea to think that fellatio is not having sexual relations with someone, but he got away with it.

Filegate. In 1993 a man named Craig Livingstone was an official in the White House office of personnel security who collected several hundred background files on Republican opponents. The assumption by many people was that he had done this on orders from Hillary, but she said that she didn't know him. Maybe she didn't. But one day in a White House hallway Hillary was spotted by an intern hugging Livingstone.

Flowers, Gennifer. One day in the middle of the 1992 New Hampshire Primary, Gennifer Flowers came out of the woodwork and told the world that she had had a romantic relationship with Bill. She said it had gone on for twelve years, while he was governor of Arkansas and married to Hillary.

Clinton denied the affair, until Flowers produced tapes where they were being lovey-dovey to each other, including calling each other honey, which Hillary said was merely a platonic term used all over Arkansas. Perhaps it was, but it was not usually accompanied by heavy breathing. The Flowers affair led to Bill and Hillary going on *60 Minutes* where they would try to salvage Clinton's rapidly sinking campaign. (See *60 Minutes* Interview).

Foster, Vince. In between adulterous affairs, Bill Clinton was making great strides as he pushed his political goals in Arkansas in the 1980s. The problem was that he didn't have much money. But Hillary did. She worked for the Rose law firm, and though cited as one of the smaller earners at the firm one year, she still raked in over $200,000.

Her confidante during those days was a brilliant lawyer named Vince Foster, one person that she trusted completely. In reading about their relationship one gets a sense that there were no secrets between them. But then a big problem occurred when Vince followed Bill and Hillary to Washington when Clinton won the presidency in 1992. Vince, who was suffering from undiagnosed depression, killed himself. Hillary reacted by removing paperwork from Vince's office, paperwork that would possibly incriminate her in many of the scandals that he was involved in. The papers turned up two years after they were requested by prosecutors, and then there was another investigation into why this occurred.

Some people believe that Hillary had Foster murdered

because he knew too much, but this is about as believable as thinking that the Mafia murdered JFK.

Fuck. A word—which most psychiatrists will tell you has a hostile connotation—that Hillary often uses when expressing her displeasure at something. It is hard to imagine a female First Lady who was more crude than Hillary. Can one imagine Eleanor Roosevelt or Ladybird Johnson saying to Secret Service or other law enforcement people, "Get the fuck out of here?"

Hillary, Sir Edmund. First man to scale Mount Everest. Hillary told a famous lie about him—that her mother named her after Sir Edmund. To make the lie more believable, she fattened it with persuasive details, like her mother had read an article about Sir Edmund when she was pregnant, and admired him. "So when I was born," Hillary said, "she called me Hillary and she always told me it's because of Sir Edmund Hillary." Later, reporters learned that since Clinton was born in 1947 the story didn't fly, because the other Hillary climbed Mount Everest on May 29, 1953—almost six years after Hillary was born.

"Investment, The Magic." This occurred after Bill Clinton became governor of Arkansas. Hillary invested the lordly sum of $1,000 with a commodities broker named Robert L "Red" Bone, and she was able to turn a $99,537 profit—in about a year. How? She said she did so by studying the *Wall Street Journal*. Author

Edward Klein says Hillary lied, that the almost $100,000 profit was facilitated by Arkansas power brokers who wanted to make sure they were in good standing with her newly-elected husband. In other words, it was a payoff, and that if they had not been behind her she would have lost all her money. The brokers who helped her get such an obscene return on her investment were later prosecuted for using the same methods to turn a big profit.

Iraq. Hillary Clinton wholeheartedly endorsed the Iraq War, but she has spent the last four or five years trying to explain that she really didn't, that President Bush did not provide her with enough information upon which she could make an informed decision. Her stance now is one of the things that has turned even Democrats against her. It is not the decision that bothers them, but her inability to own up to the truth.

Jones, Donald G. When Hillary was fourteen, thirty-year-old Don Jones came to Park Ridge and took over the job as minister. Jones possessed an expansive mission to open his students up to his view of the wider world and transform them. Transform them, as it turned out for Hillary, into a whole new way of thinking that motivated her and others on a road to the left.

Jones, Paula. A state employee in Arkansas who was led by state troopers to a hotel in Little Rock, then to a room, then through the room where she met Bill Clinton, his underwear and pants down around his ankles and with him pointing at her not with his hands, but with something else. Later, Jones sued Clinton for sexual assault and won the case, which was reversed on appeal. But Jones wouldn't go away and "Slick Willy," as the president was sometimes called, ultimately had to cough up $850,000.

Monicagate. The press moniker hung on the affair that Monica Lewinsky had with Bill Clinton where, for perhaps the first time in history, a blow job was not considered sexual relations.

Panthers, Black. Hillary started to support this group while she was in Yale Law School. It was the kind of organization that liberals typically supported, using selective thinking to believe only the good about the group, and sometimes the very bad. Founded in Oakland, California, the Panthers were constantly at war with the Oakland police and many deaths occurred, both of police and Panthers. There were also murders committed by the Panthers in other areas of the country, and ultimately its violent core brought it down.

Morris, Dick. One-time political adviser of the Clintons. Indeed, it is said that it was Morris who was the architect of Bill Clinton's run for the Presidency in 1992. But he fell out with the Clintons because he says that one day when Clinton was angry with him Bill wrestled him to the ground, which Morris found degrading.

Moynihan, Daniel Patrick. The esteemed New York State Senator whose decision not to run opened up the opportunity for Hillary. Moynihan and his wife, who was also his campaign manager, did not like Hillary but were backed into a corner. According to Edward Klein, both Moynihans felt that Hillary would do anything to get elected, and his wife in particular thought of Hillary as person who would lie about anything.

Rodham, Dorothy Howell. Hillary's mother. Like Hillary's father, she was a demanding person and had what one author characterized as a "grim" childhood which featured her, all of eight years old, traveling alone across the country with her sister.

Rodham, Hugh. Hillary's father, a tough-as-nails ex-seaman who set the bar for his children in the stratosphere. And it seemed that Hillary could never climb to where she wanted to go, because as someone once said, there is no "finish line in this quest." The presidency would seem to be as close as you could get, but the bottom line one psychiatrist was heard to say is that it's a "big, tiresome job." Only those with special motivation would seek it—like Hillary.

Tillich, Paul. Communist-inspired German theologian who Donald G. Jones believed in heart and soul. Tillich redefined Christianity in terms of the German idealistic tradition and existentialism. Jones believed that the major flaw of contemporary Christianity was its deep roots in middle-class culture. Its revival, Tillich argued, could only come from a critique of society that took its inspiration from Marxist lines of thought. In this new spin on Christianity, death and redemption were no longer the key features of theology. The major problem facing American youth, Jones said, was a crisis of meaning and alienation. This was the kind of thinking that he exposed his students to, including a teenager named Hillary Rodham.

Travelgate. One day in 1993, Hillary fired the entire staff—some of them with decades worth of experience—of the White House travel office, the people who handled lucrative travel arrangements for the press traveling with the Clintons. The ostensible reason was that an internal audit on the office found it to be grossly mismanaged; so Hillary, instead of giving the employees time to clean up their act, wielded the ax.

But as is so often the case with Hillary, many pundits said that she had an ulterior motive. According to insider David Watkins, Hillary wielded the ax so she could give the office to the Clintons' Arkansas friends Linda Bloodworth Thomason and Harry Thomason.

Tripp, Linda. Tripp encouraged Monica to tell her about her relationship with Bill and included all kinds of prurient detail, with Linda listening avidly and responding sympathetically. But Tripp taped the conversations, ending up with twenty hours worth, enough to write a book, and she also gave the copies of the tapes to Kenneth Starr, who had been appointed to investigate the Clintons role in the Whitewater debacle but expanded his investigation into the Lewinsky and Paula Jones affairs.

Village, It Takes a. Hillary Clinton's first book. Key concept: "As a society we have a choice to make. We can permit the marketplace largely to determine the values and well-being of the village, or we can continue . . . to expect business to play a social as well as an economic role."

Wellesley. Connecticut college that Hillary attended and at which she blossoms into a radical, the quintessential moment of which was a graduation day speech where she ripped into Massachusetts Attorney General Edward Brooke in an action that was a betrayal of the president of the college and was embarrassing and demeaning to Brooke. Hillary's basic contention as that the administration was not focused on the real problems of the country, and that Brooke was just playing lip service to the problems in America. It was a sort of coming out party for Hillary, the speech putting her on the cover of *Life* magazine.

Whitewater. This became a symbol of greed and duplicity. Details on Whitewater were first publicized in 1992 in the *New York Times* in a series of articles written by Jeff Gerth, and in the midst of Bill Clinton's presidential campaign, and continued throughout Hillary's time as

First Lady. It referred to a parcel of land near Flippin, Arkansas that became known as Whitewater later. The Clintons had partnered up with Jim McDougal and his wife, Susan, to develop it into housing.

It didn't work out for the Clintons; they lost their late-investment in the Whitewater Development Corporation with the McDougals, who also operated Madison Guaranty, a savings and loan institution that retained the legal services of Rose law firm—where Hillary was a partner—and may have been improperly subsidizing Whitewater losses. Madison Guaranty later failed, and Clinton's work at Rose was scrutinized for a possible conflict of interest in representing the bank before state regulators that her husband, the governor, had appointed. She claimed she had done minimal work for the bank.

Independent counsels Robert Fiske and Kenneth Starr subpoenaed Clinton's legal billing records and she claimed to be unable to produce these records. The records were found in the First Lady's White House book room after a two-year search, and delivered to investigators in early 1996. The delayed appearance of the records sparked intense interest and another investigation about how they surfaced and where they had been. Clinton attributed the problem to disorganization that resulted from their move from the Arkansas governor's mansion and the effects of a White House renovation. After the discovery of the records, Clinton made history by becoming the first First Lady to be subpoenaed to testify before a Federal grand jury.

After several Independent Counsels investigated, a final report was issued in 2000, which stated that there was insufficient evidence that either Clinton had engaged in criminal wrongdoing, but some people felt there was some involvement, but no proof. Also, Hillary denied being even involved in Whitewater in any substantial way, though ultimately it came out that she had done sixty hours worth of work on it when she had been a member of Rose law firm. To this day, Whitewater retains its stench.

Willey, Kathleen. Kathleen Willey, an attractive, one-time White House aide who, in 1993 claimed to have been groped by then-president Bill Clinton in the Oval Office. She was also on The *Fox and Friends* morning program and said she believed Clinton had had her cat Bullseye murdered, and then was accosted by another man who said he was sorry about Bullseye. Willey said that she believed this was part of an intimidation plan organized by the Clintons after she was called to testify in Paula Jones' sexual harassment suit against the president.

Bibliography

★ ★ ★ ★ ★ ★ ★ ★ ★ ★ ★ ★ ★ ★ ★ ★

BOOKS

Aldrich, Gary. *Unlimited Access: An FBI Agent Inside the Clinton White House.* Washington, DC: Regnery Publishing, Inc., 1996.

Andersen, Christopher, *American Evita: Hillary Clinton's Path to Power.* New York: William Morrow & Co., 2004.

——*Bill & Hillary: The Marriage.* New York: William Morrow & Co., 1999.

Baker, Peter. *The Breach: Inside the Impeachment and Trial of William Jefferson Clinton.* New York: Scribner, 2000.

Bork, Robert, *The Tempting of America Free Press, 1997.*

Brock, David. *The Real Anita Hill.* New York: The Free Press, 1993.

—— *The Seduction of Hillary Rodham.* New York: Simon & Schuster, 1996.

Brown, Kendall. *The Rants, Raves & Thoughts of Bill Clinton.* New York: On Your Own Publications, 2003.

Brown, L.D. *Crossfire: Witness in the Clinton Investigation.* Chula Vista, CA: Black Forest Press, 1999.

Califano, Joseph. *Inside: A Public and Private Life.* New York: Public Affairs, 2004.

Carpozi, George, Jr. *Clinton Confidential: The Climb to Power: The Unauthorized Biography of Bill and Hillary Clinton.* Del Mar, CA: Emery Dalton Books, 1995.

Clinton, Hillary. *It Takes a Village.* New York: Simon & Schuster, 1996.

—— *Living History.* New York: Scribner, 2003.

Clinton, Hillary Rodham and Claire G. Osborne. *The Unique Voice of Hillary Rodham Clinton: A Portrait in Her Own Words.* New York: Avon Books, 1997.

Clinton, William Jefferson. *My Life.* New York: Knopf Publishers, 2004.

Coulter, Ann. *High Crimes & Misdemeanors: The Case Against Bill Clinton.* Washington, D.C.: Regnery Publishing, Inc., 1998.

—— *Slander: Liberal Lies About the American Right.* New York: Crown Publishers, 2002.

Dumas, Ernest. *The Clintons of Arkansas,* 1993, U of Arkansas.

Elder, J. *Showdown: Confronting Bias, Lies, and the Special Interests that Divide America.* New York: St. Martin's Press, 2002.

Gergen, David. *Eyewitness to Power: The Essence of Leadership, Nixon to Clinton.* New York: Simon & Schuster, 2000.

Gielow, Fred. *You Don't Say: Sometimes Liberals Show Their True Colors.* Boca Raton, FL: Freedom Books, 1999.

Graham, Tim. *Pattern of Deception: The Media's Role in the Clinton Presidency.* Washington, D.C.: Media Research Center, 1996.

Gross, Martin L. *The Great Whitewater Fiasco.* New York: Ballantine Books, 1994.

Hannity, Sean. *Let Freedom Ring: Winning the War of Liberty Over Liberalism.* New York: Harper Collins, 2002.

Harris, John F. *The Survivor: Bill Clinton in the White House.* New York: Random House, 2005.

Hastert, Dennis. *Speaker: Lessons from Forty Years in Coaching and Politics.* Washington, DC: Regnery Publishing, Inc., 2004.

Hayward, Stephen. *The Real Jimmy Carter: How Our Worst Ex-President Undermines American Foreign Policy, Coddles Dictators, and Created the Party of Clinton and Kerry.* Washington, D.C.: Regnery Publishing, Inc., 2004.

Hubbell, Webb. *Friends in High Places: Our Journey From Little Rock to Washington, D.C.* New York: William Morrow & Co., 1997.

Ingraham, Laura. *The Hillary Trap: Looking for Power in All the Wrong Places.* New York: Hyperion, 2000.

Isikoff, Michael. *Uncovering Clinton: A Reporter's Story.* New York: Crown Publishers, 1999.

Kessler, Ronald. *A Matter of Character: Inside the White House of George W. Bush.* New York: Sentinel Books, 2004.

——*Inside the White House.* New York: Pocket, 1996.

Klein, Ed. *The Truth About Hillary: What She Knew, When She Knew It, and How Far She'll Go to Become President.* New York: Sentinel, 2005.

Kuiper, Thomas D. *I've Always Been a Yankee Fan: Hillary Clinton in Her Own Words.* Los Angeles, World Ahead Publishing, 2006.

Kurtz, Howard. *Spin Cycle: How the White House and the Media Manipulate the News.* New York: Free Press, 1998.

Limbacher, Carl. *Hillary's Scheme: Inside the Next Clinton's Ruthless Agenda to Take the White House.* New York: Crown Forum, 2003.

Limbaugh, David. *Absolute Power: The Legacy of Corruption in the Clinton-Reno Justice Department.* Washington, D.C. Regnery Publishing, Inc., 2001.

Lowry, Rich. *Legacy: Paying The Price for the Clinton Years.* Washington, D.C.: Regnery Publishing, Inc., 2003.

Maraniss, David. *First in His Class: A Biography of Bill Clinton.* New York: Simon & Schuster, 1995.

Matalin, Mary and James Carville. *All's Fair: Love, War, and Running For President.* New York: Random House, 1994.

McDougal, Jim and Curtis Wilkie. *Arkansas Mischief: The*

Birth of a National Scandal. New York: Henry Holt & Company, 1998.

Medved, Michael. *Right Turns: Unconventional Lessons from a Controversial Life.* New York: Crown Forum Publishers, 2004.

Milton, Joyce. *The First Partner: Hillary Rodham Clinton.* New York: William Morrow & Co., 1999.

Morris, Dick, *Behind the Oval Office,* Renaissance Books, 1998.

—— *Rewriting History.* New York: Regan Books, 2004.

Morris, Roger. *Partners in Power: The Clintons and Their America.* New York: Henry Holt & Company, 1996.

Noonan, Peggy. *The Case Against Hillary Clinton.* New York: Regan Books, 2000.

Oakley, Meredith. *On the Make: The Rise of Bill Clinton.* Washington, D.C.: Regnery Publishing, Inc., 1994.

Olson, Barbara. *Hell to Pay: The Unfolding Story of Hillary Rodham Clinton.* Washington, DC: Regnery Publishing, Inc., 1999.

—— *The Final Days: The Last, Desperate Abuses of Power by the Clinton White House.* Washington, D.C.: Regnery Publishing, Inc., 2001.

Oppenheimer, Jerry. *The State of a Union: Inside the Complex Marriage of Bill and Hillary Clinton.* New York: Harper Collins Publishing, 2000.

O'Reilly, Bill. *The No Spin Zone: Confrontations with the Powerful and Famous in America.* New York: Broadway Books, 2001.

Patterson, Lt. Col. Robert "Buzz." *Dereliction of Duty: The Eyewitness Account of How Bill Clinton Endangered America's Long-Term National Security.* Washington, D.C.: Regnery Publishing, Inc., 2003.

—— *Reckless Disregard: How Liberal Democrats Undercut Our Military, Endanger Our Soldiers, and Jeopardize Our Security.* Washington, D.C.: Regnery Publishing Inc., 2004.

Posner, Gerald L. *Why America Slept: The Failure to Prevent 9/11.* New York: Random House, 2003.

Rodcliffe, Donnie. *Hillary Rodham Clinton: A First Lady for Our Time.* New York: Warner Books, 1993.

Ruddy, Christopher and Carl Limbacher, Jr., eds., *Bitter Legacy: Newsmax.com Reveals the Untold Story of the Clinton-Gore Years.* West Palm Beach, FL: NewsMaxMedia, 2001.

—— *Hillary Clinton's Plans for the Presidency: Know The Real Hillary! The Story The Media Won't Report.* NewsMax.com, 2001.

Sheehy, Gail. *Hillary's Choice.* New York: Ballantine Publishing Group, 1999.

Stephanopoulos, George. *All Too Human.* New York: Little Brown & Co., 1999.

Stewart, James. *Blood Sport: The Truth Behind the Scandals in the Clinton White House.* New York: Simon & Schuster, 1996.

Toobin, Jeffrey. *A Vast Conspiracy: The Real Story of the Sex Scandal that Nearly Brought Down a President.* New York: Random House, 1999.

Tyrell, R. Emmett. *Boy Clinton: A Political Biography.* Washington, D.C.: Regnery Publishing, Inc., 1996.

—— *Madame Hillary: The Dark Road to the White House.* Washington, D.C.: Regnery Publishing, Inc., 2004.

Warner, Judith, *The Inside Story* New York, Signet 1999

Woodward, Bob. *Shadow: Five Presidents and the Legacy of Watergate.* New York: Simon & Schuster, 1999.

—— *The Agenda: Inside the Clinton White House.* New York: Simon & Schuster, 1994.

NEWSPAPERS AND MAGAZINES

American Heritage
American Spectator
Arkansas Democrat Gazette
Associated Press
Boston Globe
Business Week
Crains Insider
Harper's
Investors Business Daily
Ladies Home Journal
National Review
New Republic
New York Daily News
New York Post
New York Times
New York Times Magazine

New Yorker
Newsday
NewsMax
Newsweek
People
Philadelphia Enquirer
Richmond Times Dispatch
Time
U.S. News & World Report
USA Today
Vanity Fair
Wall Street Journal
Washington Post
Yale Review of Law and Social Action